# A MONTH OF SUNDAYS

AMBER LANE PRESS

*For Trisha and Matthew with love*

All rights whatsoever in this play are strictly reserved and application for performance etc. should be made before rehearsal to:

Lemon and Durbridge Ltd.
24 Pottery Lane
London W11 4LZ

No performance may be given unless a licence has been obtained.

First published in 1986, reprinted 1990 by
Amber Lane Press Ltd.
Church Street
Charlbury, Oxford OX7 3PR

Printed in Great Britain by
Athenaeum Press Ltd, Newcastle-on-Tyne

Copyright © Bob Larbey, 1986
ISBN: 0 906399 69 6

CONDITIONS OF SALE
This book is sold subject to the condition that it shall not, by way of trade or otherwise, be lent, re-sold, hired out or otherwise circulated without the publisher's prior consent in any form of binding or cover other than that in which it is published and without a similar condition including this condition being imposed on the subsequent purchaser.

# CHARACTERS

AYLOTT
COOPER
JULIA
PETER
MRS. BAKER
NURSE WILSON

The action of the play takes place in Cooper's room in a Rest Home for the Elderly on the first Sunday in April and the first Sunday in May.

*A Month of Sundays* was first presented by arrangement with H.M. Tennent Ltd. under the title of *The First Sunday in Every Month* at the Nuffield Theatre, Southampton on 14th November, 1985. It was directed by Justin Greene with the following cast:

| | |
|---|---|
| AYLOTT: | Geoffrey Bayldon |
| COOPER: | George Cole |
| JULIA: | Maggie Henderson |
| PETER: | Edward Lyon |
| MRS. BAKER: | Lorraine Peters |
| NURSE WILSON: | Siobhán Redmond |

Designer: Sarah-Jane McClelland
Lighting Designer: Dave Horn

*A Month of Sundays* transferred to the Duchess Theatre, London on 7th February, 1986.

# ACT ONE

# SCENE ONE

*The room is large, and on the first floor of what looks to be a Victorian country house, but the furniture is modern and the decor bright and attractive.*

*Upstage almost the entire wall is taken up with large leaded windows. The head of the bed is against the windows. By the bed is a bedside locker and an upright chair.*

*A door leads off Stage Right to the corridor. Against this wall is a wardrobe and some shelves containing books and a few personal effects.*

*Another door leads off Stage Left to the bathroom. Against this wall is a dressing table with another upright chair in front of it.*

*Downstage is a coffee table and two armchairs.*

*It is an early April morning and the room is gradually getting lighter.*

*COOPER, in pyjamas and dressing gown, sits in one of the armchairs. The bed has been slept in.*

*COOPER is in his late sixties — rather frail but lively of mind.*

COOPER: The Panzers will be coming soon. They're in the kitchen now, loading up for the first offensive of the day. Fuel on board — tea, coffee, orange juice. Ammunition on board — porridge, cereals, eggs, bacon, armour-piercing sausages. The crews stand ready, smart and starched. Then a signal from the Divisional Commander, Mrs. Simmons, and they rumble out into the corridors, cutting a swathe of clatter through the silence of an early morning. There's little resistance — the odd cry of, 'I don't want any breakfast.' Quite useless — the breakfast is left in any case. 'I don't want any breakfast' is translated as meaning, 'But nevertheless I do want to lie here looking at the breakfast I don't want to eat.' Some of course — the Zombies — aren't really sure which meal it is they're supposed to be eating. That's a victory of sorts, I suppose. At least it robs the Panzers of the satisfaction of knowing that their dawn Blitzkrieg has been a total success. They can hardly triumph at someone eating his breakfast when that someone is quite convinced he's eating his lunch. My friend Aylott once devised an ingenious plan. He dropped his upper dentures into his scrambled eggs. The dentures were retrieved and of course the scrambled eggs were taken away and just for that morning, the Panzers forgot to bring him back a fresh plateful. We formed an Escape Committee last summer, Aylott and I. It entailed causing a huge explosion of porridge in the kitchen and Aylott and I making our way to Switzerland disguised as nuns. He was much better in the summer, Aylott.

[*He hears a noise in the corridor.*]

Ah, the Panzers!

[*There is a tap at the door.*]

[*loudly*] I should think twice, Fritz! I've got a twenty-five pounder trained on the door!

[NURSE WILSON *enters with a breakfast tray. She is about 24.*]

WILSON: Good morning, Mr. Cooper.
COOPER: [*putting his hands up*] Kamerad!

[WILSON *puts the tray down and goes to draw the curtains behind the bed.*]

WILSON: If you must get up so early, why don't you sit by the window?
COOPER: I've seen the window.
WILSON: You've got a lovely view.
COOPER: I've seen the view.
WILSON: Eat your breakfast whilst it's hot.
COOPER: To do that, Wilson, I'd have to perch on your trolley as you leave the kitchens. [*taking the cover off his main dish*] I do believe that's scrambled egg.
WILSON: You asked for scrambled egg.
COOPER: In that case, *mea culpa*.

[WILSON *starts to make his bed.*]

I hope you're tucking those covers in nice and tight.

## ACT ONE, SCENE ONE

WILSON: Why?
COOPER: It would spoil the nightly challenge if I could get into bed easily. Of course, if you made the bed with me in it, I'd never get out of bed in the first place.
WILSON: Don't tempt me.
COOPER: I dreamt about you again last night, Wilson. You were quite naked.
WILSON: Now there's a surprise.
COOPER: Except . . .
WILSON: Except?
COOPER: Except for a long rope of pearls swinging between your full breasts.
WILSON: I haven't got full breasts.
COOPER: It *was* a dream.
WILSON: I'm not exactly flat-chested.
COOPER: Ah!
WILSON: I don't know why I listen to you.
COOPER: Because we talk of today. We talk of beautiful things like your fairly full breasts. It's better than senile mumblings or tales of an age before you were born. Those are tights, aren't they?
WILSON: Yes.
COOPER: Shame on you.
WILSON: You really are a dirty old man.
COOPER: Now that's a point. When does one become a dirty old man? You never hear anyone talk of a dirty young man — or a dirty middle-aged man. It's as though 'dirty' and 'old' are synonymous. I shall write to *The Times*.
WILSON: My fella works for *The Times*.
COOPER: Is he on strike?
WILSON: No he isn't!
COOPER: Makes a change. How's Aylott?
WILSON: He's doing very well.
COOPER: Doing what very well? Walking — thinking — breathing?
WILSON: I expect he'll be along to see you later.
COOPER: Did I tell you of the Escape Committee we formed in the summer, Aylott and I?
WILSON: Yes, you did.
COOPER: Oh shit!
WILSON: It doesn't matter.

COOPER: It does. I'd forgotten.
WILSON: It's not a crime.
COOPER: No, it's not a crime.
WILSON: In the summer, when it's warmer, I shall probably wear stockings.
COOPER: You she-devil!
WILSON: That's if you buy me that long rope of pearls.
COOPER: Done.

[WILSON *turns to go.*]

Wilson?
WILSON: Yes?
COOPER: The Escape Committee. How many times did I tell you before?
WILSON: Just once.

[COOPER *looks at her, seeking confirmation that she is telling the truth.*]

Would I lie? Would I lie? [*pleased that she has made* COOPER *smile*] I'll see you later.

[*She goes.*]

COOPER: I'm quite vain where Wilson is concerned. In fact, I've persuaded myself that I'm her little ray of sunshine. Not perhaps the brightest of rays, but that's only comparative to the Stygian darkness of most of the minds here. George Hartley joined the Zombies yesterday. Big chap — 'Remarkably fit for his age,' that's what everybody said. Visitors often mistook him for a member of the staff. He used to fuel that particular fire by wearing his blue suit quite a lot — there's something about a blue suit. Then, yesterday afternoon, big 'Remarkably fit for his age' George Hartley, complete with blue suit, was discovered paddling in the pond in the garden. Thought he was at the seaside. Then he cried.

[*He pushes his breakfast tray away and stands up, none too easily.*]

Now if I could have George Hartley's 'Remarkably fit for his age' body . . . perhaps a brain transplant. 'Medical Breakthrough in Surrey Rest Home!' [*to his own body as he walks to the window*] Will you *move*? Well, Hartley's not in the pond today — at least, not yet.

[*From outside the door comes the sound of a vacuum cleaner.*]

That will be the second Panzer wave, mopping up any pockets of resistance. Mopping up — that's quite good. I must forget that — *remember* that. Aylott and I did formulate a theory that the steady whine of vacuum cleaners could actually affect the alpha rhythms of the brain. Then I posed the question as to whether most of the brains here *had* any alpha rhythms and the whole thing petered out.

[MRS. BAKER *bustles in to clean the room. She is in her forties and works with a fierce intensity.*]

MRS. BAKER: Morning. I shan't be a minute.

COOPER: You will, Mrs. Baker, but no matter. I shall bask in the radiance of your physical beauty.

MRS. BAKER: Yes well, you want to try it.

COOPER: Try what?

MRS. BAKER: You wouldn't know where to start.

COOPER: Elliptical.

MRS. BAKER: What is?

COOPER: Your conversation.

MRS. BAKER: Meaning?

COOPER: We don't communicate, Mrs. Baker.

MRS. BAKER: Well, we all know who that is.

COOPER: Who who is? That doesn't sound right.

MRS. BAKER: There's a lot of old blokes in here who hardly know what day it is, but they don't go on like you.

COOPER: They can't go on like me.

MRS. BAKER: Well, they don't.

COOPER: We really should discuss the meaning of Life sometime, Mrs. Baker.

MRS. BAKER: Yes, yes.

COOPER: Is that you agreeing with me?

MRS. BAKER: No, it isn't.

COOPER: Then why did you say, 'Yes, yes?'

MRS. BAKER: Why you can't go for a walk while I clean your room I don't know.

COOPER: I'd miss the conversation.

MRS. BAKER: What conversation? Is this your idea of conversation? It's not mine. Now Mr. Aylott, he knows what a proper conversation is. We talk about all sorts of things, me and Mr. Aylott — outside things.

COOPER: If you mean the world beyond the gate, I can only express total disinterest.

MRS. BAKER: Well, you ought to be ashamed.

COOPER: If I can't physically get further than the gate, why should I want to know what goes on beyond it?

MRS. BAKER: Because it's the world, that's why.

COOPER: Oh, the world?

MRS. BAKER: Yes. And you can get further than the gate any time you like.

COOPER: What do you have in mind, a piggy-back?

MRS. BAKER: Hire a taxi. You've got the money.

COOPER: The equivalent of being taken for a ride in my pram.

MRS. BAKER: Oh, it's pride is it?

COOPER: You're beginning to get on my nerves.

MRS. BAKER: Well that makes a change from you getting on mine. This isn't even supposed to be one of my rooms, you know. I'm up the other end.

COOPER: But you can't stay away from me?

MRS. BAKER: Oh, I could. I could. I'm just not letting Mrs. Malik near you. You'd have her in tears.

COOPER: Or raptures.

MRS. BAKER: And that's another thing. You're sex-crazed. It's not natural in a man of your age.

COOPER: Actually, I haven't felt the physical urge for some years, but I can still remember what they were like. And until I join the Zombies, I shall enjoy doing so.

MRS. BAKER: You shouldn't call them Zombies.

COOPER: You heard about 'Remarkably fit for his age' George Hartley going for a paddle yesterday?

MRS. BAKER: Poor man.

COOPER: Why poor? He can spend his days in Wonderland now — going to the seaside.

MRS. BAKER: You're quite evil sometimes.

COOPER: Not dull?

MRS. BAKER: No, not dull.

COOPER: Praise indeed.

MRS. BAKER: Self-centred.

## ACT ONE, SCENE ONE

COOPER: Guilty.

MRS. BAKER: You could get at least two more beds in a room this size.

COOPER: I don't want two more beds in a room this size.

MRS. BAKER: Yes well, you want to try it.

COOPER: You said that before. What is it that you want me to try?

MRS. BAKER: You try looking after your father.

COOPER: Rather difficult. He's in a little urn somewhere in Wimbledon.

MRS. BAKER: You know what I mean.

COOPER: You look after your father?

MRS. BAKER: And run a family and do a job. He'd give his eye teeth for a room like this.

COOPER: Has he got any eye teeth?

MRS. BAKER: He's seventy.

COOPER: So's George Hartley and every tooth in his head is his own. I do hope he doesn't start trying to take them out and put them in a glass at night.

MRS. BAKER: You're wishing that poor man's mind away, aren't you?

COOPER: Yes I am. He cried after he paddled.

MRS. BAKER: Poor man.

COOPER: Not the tears of a child who's lost its parents on a beach. The tears of a 'Remarkably fit for his age' man who found himself paddling in the pond, wearing the blue suit that made people think he was on the staff. No-one walking past that pond would have taken him for a member of the staff, would they? Better he didn't cry. Better he waved an imaginary bucket and spade and toddled off to make some imaginary sand-castles. I'm going to have a pee.

[*He makes his way into the bathroom.* MRS. BAKER *gets on with her cleaning.*]

[*off*] I'm inhibited. Would you mind singing, Mrs. Baker?

MRS. BAKER: Don't be daft.

[*But* MRS. BAKER *does start to sing, rather self-consciously. She sings 'Alice Blue Gown.' She has rather a sweet voice and, as she goes on with the song, gains confidence in it.* COOPER *comes out from the bathroom, takes* MRS. BAKER *in his arms and engages her in a slow waltz.* MRS. BAKER *does not resist and goes on with the song.* NURSE WILSON *comes in to see the last of this. When* MRS. BAKER *sees her, she breaks off.*]

We were dancing.

COOPER: Tell the world, Wilson! We're in love!

MRS. BAKER: Fool.

[*Seeing that* COOPER *is out of breath,* WILSON *pushes a chair close to him. Quite deliberately,* COOPER *makes his way to a chair further away and sits down.*]

WILSON: I didn't know you could sing, Mrs. Baker.

MRS. BAKER: [*gathering her equipment*] Oh, I can sing. There's no reason why I shouldn't be able to sing.

WILSON: Why don't you come round with us at Christmas?

MRS. BAKER: That's carols.

WILSON: I know.

MRS. BAKER: No. I don't like carols.

WILSON: Why?

MRS. BAKER: Because I don't.

WILSON: Oh. There's a brew-up at the nurses' station.

MRS. BAKER: Mm. I might have a cup of tea. I might do that. [*to* COOPER] I'll see you tomorrow.

COOPER: 'Ye Gods! Annihilate but space and time, And make two lovers happy!'

MRS. BAKER: Yes. I thought you'd have something funny to say.

[*She goes.* WILSON *takes* COOPER's *pulse.*]

COOPER: Now what are you doing that for?

[WILSON *does a little shake of the head.*]

Of course, you're counting. I must remember that. Antidote for chattering nurses — make them take your pulse a lot. Well?

WILSON: You just had to walk to this chair, didn't you?

COOPER: You can't simply plonk yourself down on the ballroom floor. It spoils the moment.

WILSON: You shouldn't get out of breath.

COOPER: Indeed I shouldn't, Wilson. Dangerous habit. I have it on very good authority that if you get completely out of breath, you keel over and shuffle off the old mortal coil. I'm peeing more, you know.

## ACT ONE, SCENE ONE

WILSON: Don't worry about that. You've done very well with your breakfast.

COOPER: Does that describe the amount eaten, or the aesthetic arrangement of what I have left?

WILSON: What would you like for lunch? The beef or the chicken?

COOPER: Which do you recommend?

WILSON: The chicken.

COOPER: I'll have the beef.

WILSON: Would you like me to bring you up a newspaper?

COOPER: No thank you.

WILSON: Or you could pop down and get one yourself.

COOPER: You never give up, do you?

WILSON: It was only a fall.

COOPER: I couldn't have had it in the privacy of my own room, could I?

WILSON: You're not the only person it's ever happened to.

COOPER: And that's another thing. Why do we 'Have a fall?' Why can't people say 'He fell down?' They don't, do they? 'He had a fall.' The next time I do it — and not in the residents' lounge — I shall issue instructions that it is reported as 'Mr. Cooper went arse over tip today.'

WILSON: You're not planning one, are you?

COOPER: Only if you promise to lie beneath me.

WILSON: Your daughter comes to see you today.

COOPER: All the way from Milton Keynes. The first Sunday in every month.

WILSON: It's a long way from Milton Keynes.

COOPER: I wish I could convince her that it's too long a way altogether.

WILSON: That's not very kind.

COOPER: I'm not feeling very kind, Wilson. Since I last saw her, I've 'Had a fall,' I now have to get up twice in the night instead of once, 'Remarkably fit for his age' George Hartley has joined the Zombies and last but not least, Mrs. Baker suggests that I try looking after my father, who is in a little urn somewhere in Wimbledon.

WILSON: You do provoke her.

COOPER: I'm provoking me, Wilson. A cattle-prod to the

|        | brain. If I don't sting it, it won't work. And don't you dare say, 'For a man of your age, your brain is remarkably active.' |
|--------|---|
| WILSON: | I wasn't going to. |
| COOPER: | Oh. |
| WILSON: | I was going to say that you're feeling sorry for yourself. |
| COOPER: | My God, if I was a few years younger, your 'fella' who works for . . . |
| WILSON: | *The Times* . . . |
| COOPER: | Yes, *The Times* — I know, I know. He wouldn't stand a chance. |
| WILSON: | You'd like him. |
| COOPER: | Ah, but I *love* you. |
| WILSON: | Oh, you're crafty. |
| COOPER: | Will Aylott be along? |
| WILSON: | David and Jonathan. I must go. |

[*She picks up the breakfast tray and goes towards the door.*]

| COOPER: | Wilson? |
|---|---|
| WILSON: | What? |
| COOPER: | Would I really make Mrs. Malik cry? |
| WILSON: | Mrs. Malik? Why should you? |
| COOPER: | Mrs. Baker said I would. She said Mrs. Malik is supposed to clean this room. |
| WILSON: | She is. Mrs. Baker won't let her. You've gone quiet. |
| COOPER: | I shall think of something. |
| WILSON: | Tell me at lunch-time when I bring your chicken. |
| COOPER: | Beef! |

[WILSON *smiles and goes.* COOPER *gets up and goes to the window.*]

Daffs — daffies . . . 'I thought I saw a . . . ' or is it, 'I saw a . . . ?' What a silly name for a flower, anyway.

[AYLOTT *comes in. He is about the same age as* COOPER. *He is physically fitter and a gentler soul. He is dressed in shirt and sports jacket and carries two cups of tea.*]

Aylott!

| AYLOTT: | I cadged these from the nurses' station. |
|---|---|

[AYLOTT *sets the cups down on the coffee table. He*

## ACT ONE, SCENE ONE

*and* COOPER *take an armchair each and toast each other with the tea.*]

COOPER: The Escape Committee!
AYLOTT: The Escape Committee!
COOPER: And how are we feeling today?
AYLOTT: Oh, much the same — mustn't grumble. How are *we* feeling today?
COOPER: Oh, much the same — mustn't grumble.
AYLOTT: Mr. Spears came to see us yesterday.
COOPER: Did he? Was he pleased with us?
AYLOTT: Excellent recovery — quite a serious operation for a man of our age, he said.
COOPER: I always call him 'Doctor' instead of 'Mister.' He hates that.
AYLOTT: How are the water-works?
COOPER: Rather like your diet — little and often.
AYLOTT: What does Mr. Spears say?
COOPER: He does quite a lot of 'Ah wells.' Actually, I think he's taking mental measurements for when I have to be fitted with the dreaded bags. I read it up. You get no warning, apparently. I mean, you don't feel that you want to pee. You just do. Not very much. You're sitting there and the first you know of it is a warm trickle — and incontinence is your new companion.
AYLOTT: It could be years away.
COOPER: Not from the sound of Spears' 'Ah wells.' I'm not sure that I wouldn't sooner go paddling. Any sign of Hartley this morning, incidentally?
AYLOTT: Yes, he was . . . Where did I see him? Yes, in the lounge earlier, reading a paper.
COOPER: Upside down?
AYLOTT: They're having his blue suit cleaned apparently.
COOPER: These bags of mine.
AYLOTT: It's only one bag.
COOPER: No, that's just it. I think I shall design my own. Designer urine bags — two-legged jobs — ankle-length — save all the changing.
AYLOTT: You'd look as though you had rather fat legs.
COOPER: I wonder if I could get them sponsored — like a racing driver's suit.

AYLOTT: I think they'd want them on view.
COOPER: Yes. You don't think Dunlop or Pirelli would settle for the odd flash?
AYLOTT: Tell you what. You could have the advertising on your trousers saying '*Under* these trousers, John Cooper's urine bags are sponsored by . . .'
COOPER: No, it's not really commercially viable, is it? I think the answer may be to dispense with trousers altogether and design the bags to look like trousers.
AYLOTT: If you could make them inflatable, you could float over London like the Goodyear airship.
COOPER: We could be on to something there.
AYLOTT: We could.

[*Pleased with their sally into the surreal, they lean back in their chairs.*]

Is your daughter coming to see you today?
COOPER: First Sunday in every month.
AYLOTT: I know it's the first Sunday in the month! It was a rhetorical question.
COOPER: All right Aylott, all right.
AYLOTT: Sorry.
COOPER: I know.
AYLOTT: They say you don't notice. They say. They say that little errors start to creep in — little lapses of memory. But you *do* know — belatedly sometimes, but you do know. You're telling a story to somebody and all of a sudden you know that you've told it to them before. Not a long time ago, that would be excusable — but a short time — like yesterday.
COOPER: You didn't tell me this yesterday.
AYLOTT: That's not what I mean and you know it. I suppose they are right, ultimately. There must come a time when you don't know — or a moment in time. But do you know that moment? Are there millimoments within the moment?
COOPER: You're being very alliterative today.
AYLOTT: You described the onset of incontinence.
COOPER: Guessing. Guessing.
AYLOTT: 'The first warm trickle,' you said. Perhaps it's similar. Perhaps one millisecond you know and the next millisecond you don't.

COOPER: Look here, I'll strike a bargain with you. You start repeating yourself without knowing it at exactly the same time that I start peeing myself without knowing it.
AYLOTT: Tidy.
COOPER: It's classic. You can say, 'You're peeing yourself, you're peeing yourself, you're peeing yourself,' and I can say, 'Stop repeating yourself.'
AYLOTT: Without knowing you're peeing yourself at the time!
COOPER: Exactly. Jack Robertson and Sid Brown.
AYLOTT: Bill Edrich and Denis Compton.
COOPER: Dewes. Was it George or John?
AYLOTT: John — we think.
COOPER: We'll settle for John. John Dewes. Leslie Compton.
AYLOTT: Jim Sims, Jack Young.
COOPER: And Laurie Gray.
AYLOTT: It's still only ten men.
COOPER: Yes.
AYLOTT: Who *was* the eleventh?
COOPER: We can never remember. Perhaps by some strange quirk, when your memory goes, the name of that eleventh man will come back to you.
AYLOTT: As I forgot the other ten?
COOPER: Of course.
AYLOTT: It wasn't the young Fred Titmus, was it?
COOPER: No. Not in 1947.
AYLOTT: We could look this up, you know.
COOPER: No, no. It would spoil the challenge.
AYLOTT: I feel rather sorry for the chap whose name we can't remember. There he is, a member of the finest side that Middlesex have ever produced, and we can't remember his name.
COOPER: I don't expect he knows.
AYLOTT: No, there is that.
COOPER: Bit like the reindeer.
AYLOTT: What reindeer?
COOPER: Santa's reindeer. You know — Donner, Blitzen . . . that crowd.
AYLOTT: Are there eleven of them?
COOPER: I don't know.
AYLOTT: Well, why bring them up?

COOPER: Because nobody can ever remember all their names! I think we should bring George Hartley in on this conversation.
AYLOTT: I saw him this morning.
COOPER: Did you?
AYLOTT: Yes. In the lounge, reading a paper. [*realizing that he has said this before*] I think I'll go for a walk.
COOPER: Captain Oates said that — or something like it.
AYLOTT: [*getting up*] You're a fool, Cooper.
COOPER: So are you.
AYLOTT: You could lean on me.
COOPER: I'd have to get dressed.
AYLOTT: It's hardly climbing the Matterhorn.
COOPER: When I design the inflatable bags, you can pull me along behind you, like a balloon.
AYLOTT: Chat this evening?
COOPER: I rely on it.
AYLOTT: So do I.

[*He goes.* COOPER *goes over to the window again.*]

COOPER: Four months underground, a month's flowering and then weeks and weeks of bloody brown leaves, that's all that daffs are worth. Well, I suppose I could climb the Matterhorn. They do come all the way from Milton Keynes.

[*He goes to his wardrobe and opens it.*]

What shall it be? The blazer, I suppose. Gives one an air, a blazer. 'The man who wears a blazer knows where he's going.' Something to do with the shoulders. Can't get the same effect with a cardigan. Plus the badge, of course. Royal Army Service Corps. It's not called that any more. What is it now? The Royal Corps of Transport. They didn't even ask me if they could change it.

[*He takes out the blazer and inspects it.*]

We've got a full Colonel knocking about here somewhere. Ex-cavalry — calls the Service Corps 'Bloody lorry drivers.' He still calls himself Colonel — pompous old twit. Mind you, it has a ring to it. 'Good morning, Colonel. How are you today, Colonel?' I suppose I could insist on being addressed as 'Second Lieutenant,' but it doesn't have the same ring. Yes, the blazer. Then if Julia brings

## ACT ONE, SCENE ONE

my grandson, I can square my shoulders and tell him stories of my heroism in the Second World War. It keeps Julia quiet if I do that. I was almost a hero. [*looking out of the window*] There goes Aylott. Chin in, chest out Aylott! Don't shuffle. Good old Aylott. Oh damn. I do think I need to pee again.

[*He goes into his bathroom. As he does, he sings 'Alice Blue Gown' softly to himself.*]

## SCENE TWO

*Early afternoon, the same day.*

COOPER, *now dressed in his blazer and flannels, but still wearing his slippers, is asleep in his chair. His lunch tray is on the table. Most of the lunch is eaten.*

WILSON *comes in and picks up the tray. Seeing he is asleep, she is going to leave quietly but changes her mind. She puts the tray down again and shakes* COOPER *gently.*

COOPER: What? Mmm? Oh, hello, Wilson.
WILSON: How was the beef?
COOPER: It went on a bit.
WILSON: The chicken was delicious.
COOPER: If news of your cruelty ever leaks out, Wilson, the place will be swarming with television cameramen.
WILSON: I thought I'd wake you. They'll probably be here soon.
COOPER: Good, yes. I don't like being caught asleep. I don't like the thought of being looked at when I can't look back.
WILSON: Is there anything you want?
COOPER: Yes, I wouldn't mind it being tomorrow.
WILSON: It's a long drive from Milton Keynes.
COOPER: So you keep saying. Still, there is one thing. Each month they're contriving to arrive just a little later. I suppose the natural progression would be for them not to get out of the car at all — quick circuit of the building — shout 'Hello Dad!' and straight back to Milton Keynes.

WILSON: Mr. Aylott never gets any visitors at all.
COOPER: Lucky old Aylott.
WILSON: Shall I bring some tea later?
COOPER: No thanks. They stop at a tea-shop on the way back. What about George Hartley?
WILSON: What about George Hartley?
COOPER: He has people come all the time.
WILSON: Yes, I know.
COOPER: Well, today's contingent are going to get a bit of a shock, aren't they? What if they turn up and Hartley's standing in the pond again?
WILSON: Not that it's any of your nosy business, but Matron's going to have a word with whoever comes.
COOPER: I hope it's not his sister. Hartley once told me that he thought his sister was mad as a hatter.
WILSON: [*unable to resist it*] I suppose they could go paddling together.
COOPER: Nice one, Wilson — nice one.
WILSON: It wasn't nice at all. It was unethical and I didn't mean it.
COOPER: This word that Matron's going to have.
WILSON: It's none of your business.
COOPER: I hope she's good at it.
WILSON: She's a very caring person.
COOPER: With big knockers.
WILSON: Yes.
COOPER: The night nurse blushes if I say things like that.
WILSON: She'll learn.
COOPER: It's funny, isn't it? George Hartley is on his way to joining the Zombies, so Matron's going to tell his visitors. Who tells him?
WILSON: It would upset him. He's quite rational today.
COOPER: Well, nobody can tell him when he's irrational, can they?
WILSON: Of course not.
COOPER: So nobody tells him at all.
WILSON: No.
COOPER: But from now on, it's an irreversible procedure, isn't it? Like whiskers. So while Hartley's mind grows its senile beard, it will continue to be carried

## ACT ONE, SCENE TWO

about by that strapping body. Pity decay can't be synchronized.
WILSON: There's not a lot wrong with your mind.
COOPER: I know. But then I don't have a strapping body.
WILSON: I shall stop talking to you if you're going to be morbid.
COOPER: [*a conscious effort*] Do you know why I say that my father's in a little urn *somewhere* in Wimbledon?
WILSON: I haven't got time. Why?
COOPER: Well, on the first anniversary of his death, Marjorie and I thought we'd go along and pay our respects. Huge place, the crematorium. We couldn't find him. We ended up giving the flowers to the Late Edwina May Beasley, whoever she was. Marjorie said he'd have found it rather funny.
WILSON: You've never told me about your wife.
COOPER: When you've got a year or two to spare. She was my best friend, you see. The Padre assures me that she's waiting for me in Heaven. If I get there and find he's lying, I shall ask to be put on Thunderbolts.
WILSON: They should be here soon.
COOPER: I was right. They are getting a little later every month.
WILSON: Just be grateful.
COOPER: I am. I'm very grateful.
WILSON: Oh.
COOPER: Yes. The thought that you may wear stockings in the summer fills me with gratitude.

[WILSON *shakes her head at him and goes out with the tray.* COOPER *gets out of the chair with some exertion.*]

Ahh! At this rate I shall end up chair-shaped. A brisk walk, that's the thing.

[*He walks slowly round the room. He notices for the first time that he is still wearing carpet slippers.*]

Now they really set the blazer off, don't they?

[*He takes a pair of black shoes from his wardrobe and kicks off the slippers. He then wiggles his feet into the shoes and goes to sit down to tie the laces.*]

I'm damned if I will!

[*He puts one foot on a chair near the bed and goes to tie the laces, but he is unsteady on the other leg. He loses his balance, goes backwards, hits the bed with his backside and slides to the floor. His daughter* JULIA *and her husband* PETER *come in. They are both in their early forties. They both wear car coats and look very Milton Keynes town-housey.*]

JULIA: Oh, my God! You've had a fall!
COOPER: No I'm not and no I haven't.
PETER: Now what have you been up to?
COOPER: I was a little bored so I thought I'd fling myself to the floor!
JULIA: Shall we call somebody?
COOPER: Of course not. Just give me a hand.
PETER: Right. [*to* JULIA] I'll take the head and you take the feet.
  [*They move towards him.*]
COOPER: You haven't got the faintest idea, have you?
PETER: I'm not trained.
JULIA: We can't leave you there.
COOPER: Then give me a hand. Not you — him!
  [PETER *comes awkwardly to him.*]
PETER: I don't want to hurt you.
COOPER: Just put that arm round there. That's it. Don't dig your fingers in! Now let me get hold of your arm.
JULIA: If I crawled behind you, I could act as a support.
COOPER: If you crawled behind me, you'd be under the bed. Peter can manage. That's it. Now don't pull — just take the weight. Good.
  [*With* PETER *doing as he is told,* COOPER *manages to get to his feet.*]
PETER: Where would you like to go now?
  [COOPER *motions towards an armchair.*]
COOPER: There. Over there.
  [PETER, *still holding* COOPER'*s arm, sets off at a snail's pace.*]
  I should like to get to the chair before nightfall.
JULIA: What were you doing, anyway?
COOPER: Trying to tie my shoe-laces.
JULIA: What's wrong with your slippers?
COOPER: Slippers with a blazer?

## ACT ONE, SCENE TWO

JULIA: There's nobody to see.
COOPER: You mean I'm alone. I've joined the Zombies!
JULIA: I do wish you wouldn't use that expression.
[COOPER *gets to the armchair and lowers himself into it.*]
PETER: Don't upset your father, Julia. Would you like me to tie your shoe-laces, Dad?
COOPER: I'd be obliged. Just one knot.
JULIA: All this fuss about shoe-laces. They're perfectly nice slippers. Why you had to put shoes on I don't know. Why did you have to put shoes on?
COOPER: Because I intend to tap-dance on the table later and you don't get the same effect with slippers!
JULIA: Ooh!
PETER: Come on, come on.
COOPER: Where? Where?
PETER: Don't let's get the visit off on the wrong foot.
[COOPER *laughs.*]
Why are you laughing?
COOPER: 'Wrong foot.' Rather good, that.
PETER: Oh. Yes.
JULIA: I didn't mean to shout. We had an awful drive down and then I find you lying on the floor.
COOPER: Well, I'm all right now.
JULIA: You're sure?
COOPER: Truly.
JULIA: You haven't started having falls?
COOPER: No, I haven't started having falls.
JULIA: [*taking a bunch of daffs from her bag*] I brought you these. They're from the garden.
COOPER: Daffodils. How nice.
JULIA: I'll put them in water.
[JULIA *takes a vase and goes into the bathroom.* PETER *has been walking about the room but now feels it is his duty to pick up the conversation.*]
PETER: Sorry we were a bit late. Doesn't get any easier, that drive.
COOPER: Road-works?
PETER: Single-lane traffic for over four miles.
COOPER: What about getting back?
PETER: I think I'll try the A.5.

COOPER: I should leave a little early if I were you.
PETER: I wouldn't mind doing that, actually.
  [JULIA *comes out of the bathroom with the daffodils in a vase.*]
  Dad was just suggesting that we might leave a little early.
JULIA: We'll leave at our normal time.
PETER: I was thinking of the traffic.
JULIA: It was bad coming. Were there road-works on the north-bound lanes?
PETER: Further down, yes. I was saying that we might try the A.5. going back.
JULIA: That's a lottery.
COOPER: I should go now if I were you.
JULIA: There's no need to be sarcastic, Dad. You don't *have* that drive.
COOPER: That's true.
PETER: No, I think we should stay till our normal time.
COOPER: You didn't bring Gary?
JULIA: No. He's all right. Peter's mother is staying.
  [JULIA *sits.* PETER *continues to prowl.*]
  Do sit *down*, Peter!
PETER: I was just admiring the grounds. It really is a very nice place, isn't it?
COOPER: I should get your father's name on the waiting list.
JULIA: Dad!
PETER: No, you do have to consider these things. None of us get any younger, do we?
JULIA: It's hardly imminent.
PETER: One hopes not, naturally.
COOPER: There would be one problem.
PETER: What's that?
COOPER: The drive.
PETER: That's true.
COOPER: Why didn't you bring Gary?
JULIA: He's sorry he couldn't come. He's got his mock O-levels this term, you see.
COOPER: Ah.
JULIA: He's doing very well at school.
PETER: Bit of a mathematician, our Gary.
COOPER: Studying hard?
JULIA: He doesn't need telling.

## ACT ONE, SCENE TWO

COOPER: Even on Sundays?

JULIA: Yes.

COOPER: I thought English Lit. was his favourite subject.

PETER: Favourite, yes. But we try to steer him towards the Maths side. Infinitely more practical these days.

JULIA: He'll still take English Literature of course. He's doing 'The Knight's Tale' from *The Canterbury Tales* this term.

COOPER: 'A very parfitt gentle knight.' Parfitt. Left-hander. He played for Middlesex. Much later though.

PETER: The cricket team.

JULIA: Oh.

COOPER: Does he enjoy Chaucer?

JULIA: Oh yes.

COOPER: Good.

PETER: But at the end of the day you see, is Chaucer really going to get you anywhere?

COOPER: It depends where you want to go. Does Gary study every Sunday?

PETER: It's the mock O-levels coming up, you see.

JULIA: And he couldn't read in the car. It makes him sick. Perhaps next time.

COOPER: Yes.

JULIA: Anyway Dad, how are you?

COOPER: Oh, much the same. Mustn't grumble.

JULIA: What about your friend, Mr. Aylott?

COOPER: Oh, much the same. Mustn't grumble.

JULIA: I do wish you'd talk to me!

COOPER: I am.

JULIA: You're not. You're just making noises.

COOPER: Then the old mind's going, because I could have sworn I was talking.

JULIA: You never tell me how you really are.

COOPER: Julia, you don't want to know how I really am.

PETER: I don't think that's very fair.

COOPER: I didn't mean that Julia doesn't *want* to know. I mean . . . Look, I'm sure we've said all this before. It's boring — very boring and I don't keep a detailed record of my physical deterioration. It wouldn't mean anything, anyway — something hardened here — something slowing down there. There's no drama about it. It just goes on.

JULIA: I wasn't asking for a detailed medical up-date. I was asking how you were in yourself.
COOPER: In myself?
PETER: In general terms.
COOPER: 'General terms' — that's much better, yes. In general terms, 'Much the same, mustn't grumble.' It's true! Well, not entirely. I do grumble but my grumbles are designed solely to show what a plucky old chap I really am. Do you understand what I'm talking about?
PETER: [*not understanding*] Yes.
COOPER: Then let's change the subject.
PETER: We've got permission for the extension.
COOPER: Well that's good, isn't it?
PETER: It will have to be flat-roofed.
COOPER: Will it?
PETER: I'm pretty deeply into Building Regs. at the moment. You see, I want the roof to be load-bearing so that we can sit on it.
COOPER: Why would you want to sit on your roof?
JULIA: *With* furniture, Dad. If we put French windows in the master bedroom, we can walk straight out onto the roof — perhaps have breakfast out there in the summer.
COOPER: I thought you had a patio.
PETER: We do, but it's over-looked.
JULIA: They're nice enough people, the Bartletts, but they do tend to do a lot of looking . . .
COOPER: Yes, I see. So the idea is for you to have breakfast on your roof so that you can look down on the Bartletts.
JULIA: We shan't look down!
COOPER: Let's just hope that the Bartletts don't build an extension that's higher than yours, because you'd have to build up again then. It could go on, couldn't it? The whole of Milton Keynes could be riveted by the sight of two families eating breakfast on two enormously high towers!
[*Neither* JULIA *nor* PETER *is taken with this vision.*]
Aylott would like that. We were designing a pair of inflatable urine bags this morning.
JULIA: I'm not shocked.

## ACT ONE, SCENE TWO

COOPER: You're not laughing either.

JULIA: No wonder Gary doesn't want to come and see you!
*[She instantly regrets saying this.]*

COOPER: If you pretend you didn't say it, I'll pretend I didn't hear it.

JULIA: I didn't mean to say it.

COOPER: Will you excuse me? I seem to be in need of a pee.
*[He gets up and goes towards the bathroom.]*
Mrs. Baker sings. You don't fancy a quick burst of 'Land of Hope and Glory,' do you?
*[When COOPER has gone, PETER looks accusingly at JULIA.]*

JULIA: He made me angry.
*[PETER shakes his head disapprovingly.]*
We can't all have perfect relationships with our parents!
*[PETER gets up and goes over to the window. They do not speak. COOPER comes out of the bathroom. He sits down and starts to unlace his shoes.]*
What are you doing?

COOPER: I'm putting my slippers on. Would you mind, Peter?

PETER: Yes, of course.
*[PETER brings his slippers.]*

COOPER: Whilst you're up, Peter, there's a cardigan in the wardrobe.
*[PETER gets the cardigan.]*

JULIA: I'm sorry, Dad. He didn't want to come. I tried to persuade him, but he didn't want to come.

PETER: He's only a child.

COOPER: *[swapping his cardigan for the blazer]* Yes, I had noticed. It's all right. It's nothing more than a dented ego.

JULIA: It's not that he doesn't love you, but he started having very bad dreams.

COOPER: If I were Hartley, I'd probably understand that.

PETER: Who's Hartley?

COOPER: The local beach-comber. It doesn't matter. How could I frighten him? The last time he came all we did was select our World Cricket Eleven. I can't accept that preferring Benaud to Gibbs is frightening.

JULIA: No.

COOPER: The war stories? A Second Lieutenant in the Royal Army Service Corps who never fired a shot in anger and was invalided out with piles? Well, come on — tell me.

PETER: We're not blaming you. I don't think you know you're doing it sometimes.

COOPER: God help your clients if your legal advice is as clear as that. What don't I know I'm doing?

JULIA: You talk of death.

COOPER: I do not.

JULIA: Urine bags and Zombies and walking-frames... It crawls through every conversation like a black worm.

PETER: That's what the dreams were about.

JULIA: He started feeling that this was a place where everybody was dying.

COOPER: Well, we are.

JULIA: He doesn't want you to die.

COOPER: He's a bright enough boy. He must know about death.

JULIA: Of course he knows about death, but he's too young to be thinking of all the steps — and that's what you will talk about — all the steps — all the mess — all the decay.

COOPER: He's laughed.

JULIA: Here, yes.

PETER: He's started asking my mother some very embarrassing questions about her stomach.

COOPER: And what do you say? 'Don't be nosy, Gary. Granny's just got a nasty old tummy-ache?'

PETER: No. But I don't tell him that it could be cancer either.

COOPER: Is it?

PETER: No, it's not, as a matter of fact. I was just making a point.

COOPER: Oh.

JULIA: And the point we're trying to make...

COOPER: It's all right. It's taken.

JULIA: I am sorry.

COOPER: No, no. In any case, a lad of his age should be able to find something better to do with himself than... Has he got a girl-friend?

JULIA: Yes.
COOPER: Good for him. A nice girl?
JULIA: She wears glasses.
COOPER: My first girl-friend had a definite cast in one eye, but it didn't damp my ardour one jot.
JULIA: You're all right?
COOPER: Yes, of course. Looking forward to my tea, as a matter of fact.
PETER: We'll get something on the way home. Talking of which . . .
JULIA: We really should be going.
PETER: Not knowing what the A.5's going to be like.
JULIA: We'll stay longer if you want us to.
PETER: Yes. Give it another quarter of an hour by all means.
COOPER: No, no — you'd get into the evening traffic then.
JULIA: You're sure?
COOPER: Give Gary my love. Tell him I'm very well — I went for quite a long walk this morning — and I'm sticking with Benaud for our World Cricket Eleven.
PETER: Somebody will be looking in on you later?
COOPER: I almost have to charge admission.
PETER: The fall, I mean. Nothing's hurting?
COOPER: No, nothing's hurting.
JULIA: We'll see you next month, then. It won't seem long.
COOPER: No.
JULIA: Goodbye then, Dad. [*kissing him*] Look after yourself.
COOPER: Goodbye, Julia.
PETER: Cheerio, Dad.
COOPER: Goodbye, Peter. Good luck with the A.5.
PETER: Thanks.
JULIA: Bye. Bye.

[JULIA *and* PETER *go.* COOPER *sighs — there is some relief in the sigh.*]

COOPER: It's not that they're bad people. Peter's quite a nice chap in a droning sort of way, and Julia . . . well, 'Not her father's daughter,' as they say. Not her mother's either. Of us but somehow never ours. I sometimes have the nasty suspicion that I only loved her because I was supposed to love her. Po-faced little thing she was. Very obedient — very correct — contented rather than happy. When I think of Marjorie laughing . . .

[WILSON *comes in. She has her cloak on.*]

WILSON: I thought I'd pop in before I go off.

COOPER: Look here, Wilson, I can't have you barging in like this. You could have interrupted a very moving family scene.

WILSON: I saw them go.

COOPER: Oh.

[WILSON *sits down.*]

What are you doing?

WILSON: Taking the weight off my legs.

TOGETHER: And very nice legs they are too.

WILSON: Do you mind?

COOPER: *Mind?* Of course, if word gets out that I'm actually being visited by the delicious Nurse Wilson, I shall be lynched. 'Senile Lynch Mob Run Amok in Surrey!'

WILSON: You're not senile.

COOPER: Victim's last words. 'I am not senile. I just couldn't run.'

WILSON: They didn't stay long.

COOPER: No. New ploy. They brought the A.5. into the game. They're not only arriving later, they're finding reasons for leaving earlier.

WILSON: What did you talk about?

COOPER: Oh, we covered a good part of the intellectual spectrum. The A.5. — extensions with flat roofs — how am I in myself? That's another thing. The pauses get longer. When I used to visit Marjorie there was never enough time — until there was no time at all.

[WILSON *gets up.*]

Don't go.

WILSON: I'm not. That's the tea-trolley.

COOPER: I don't want anything to eat. Just a cup of tea.

WILSON: All right.

[WILSON *goes into the corridor and comes back with two cups of tea and some sandwiches on a plate.*]

COOPER: I said I didn't want anything to eat.

## ACT ONE, SCENE TWO

WILSON: They're for me. I'm starving.

[WILSON *sits down, gives* COOPER *his cup of tea, takes her own and tucks into the sandwiches.*]

COOPER: Taking the food from the mouth of a poor old man.

WILSON: Want one?

COOPER: I'm on to you, you know. You'll be saying, 'Open the tunnel, here comes the train,' next.

WILSON: They're very good.

COOPER: Just one, then. So long as you know I'm on to you.

WILSON: I do. I do.

[COOPER *takes a bite of a sandwich and they settle back in silence for a moment.*]

COOPER: Not bad.

WILSON: Another one?

COOPER: No thanks.

WILSON: They didn't bring your grandson today.

COOPER: No. Busy studying for his mock O-Levels apparently.

WILSON: I used to get stomach-ache before exams.

COOPER: He wanted to come, of course, but if he intends to be as grindingly successful as his father, he must study. He didn't want to come at all. I've been giving him nightmares apparently. You're supposed to say, 'I find that very hard to believe.'

WILSON: Some children do react badly to places like this.

COOPER: Really?

WILSON: Yes, really.

COOPER: It's not just me, then?

WILSON: Did they say it was?

COOPER: Yes, they did actually.

WILSON: Would you like me to have a word with them next month?

COOPER: The thought of you as a warrior maiden battling on my behalf is very exciting, Wilson, but no thank you. I suppose my sense of humour is on the mordant side, but I really thought I was amusing the boy. It is a long way to come. That's the trouble, you see — in the best of possible worlds, one should really be all things to all visitors. They're the ones who don't really know what to say because when all's said and done, what is there to say? What I should actually do is cater for all tastes. Tell my grandson funny, harmless little stories — the sort that old men are supposed to tell — reassure Julia endlessly that I'm really very well in myself and read up on extensions with flat roofs for Peter. Can't be done, can it? Can it?

WILSON: It's not your job. It's theirs.
COOPER: Ah, my warrior maiden! Hair streaming in the wind — spear in hand — 36B breastplate shining.
WILSON: How do you know I'm 36B?
COOPER: I guessed.
WILSON: They *should* understand.
COOPER: Did Hartley's relatives understand?
WILSON: We're not talking about Mr. Hartley's relatives.
COOPER: Did Matron have that chat?
WILSON: Yes. Look, your grandson's nightmares — they'll pass.
COOPER: He's got a girl-friend.
WILSON: Then they will pass.
COOPER: Better things to dream about?
WILSON: I should hope so.
COOPER: Wetly.
WILSON: You didn't have to say that.
COOPER: Shouldn't you be going?
WILSON: Soon.
COOPER: How long are you off for?
WILSON: Till Tuesday.
COOPER: Will you be seeing your young man?
WILSON: We live together.
COOPER: Wilson!
WILSON: Now don't pretend you're shocked.
COOPER: I'm not, I'm jealous. Is he kind?
WILSON: Very.
COOPER: Good-looking?
WILSON: Well . . . not particularly.
COOPER: Good. Handsome men can be very vain, you know. Look at me. You'd better go.
WILSON: Yes.

[*But* WILSON *is reluctant to go. She stands up, then quite suddenly begins to cry.*]

COOPER: Not you, Wilson — anybody but you.

[*He tries to get up but the fall has stiffened him.*]

Oh sod, sod, sod!

## ACT ONE, SCENE TWO 33

[WILSON *motions to him to stay where he is. Instead she goes and sits on the floor and rests her head on his knee.* COOPER *puts an arm round her shoulders.*]

What is it? What is it? It isn't something I said?

[WILSON *shakes her head, then composes herself a little.*]

WILSON: Remember I told you that Matron was going to have a talk with Mr. Hartley's visitors?

COOPER: Yes.

WILSON: His sister came. I took her to Matron and Matron asked me to stay. It was a beautiful talk.

COOPER: Go on.

WILSON: Mr. Hartley's sister listened. She didn't say anything. I thought perhaps it was shock. Then Matron finished and Mr. Hartley's sister — quite calmly — said she wouldn't be coming again. 'No point,' she said. That's what she said as she left — 'No point.' How can I give hope when relatives abandon it so easily?

COOPER: Oh my dear Wilson, you don't give hope. You can't because there isn't any. You give cheer and kindness and Hartley's loony sister can't diminish that.

WILSON: She wasn't loony. She just switched off as though Mr. Hartley wasn't a proper person any more.

COOPER: Look, we've seen Hartleys before. There's no road back, is there? Today he'll wonder why she didn't come. Next week or next month he might not recognize her if she did come.

WILSON: Well, I'm not letting go. Even when he doesn't know who I am, I'm not letting go. I'll smile at him and I'll make jokes to him and I'll always call him Mr. Hartley. And if just once — even for a few minutes — he knows who he is or who I am I'll phone his bloody sister and I'll say, 'There is a point. For a few minutes he was a proper person and he was treated like a proper person. There is a point!' Your knee's very knobbly.

[WILSON *gets up and repairs the damage.*]

COOPER: Well, your eyes are puffy.

WILSON: Are they?

COOPER: How long do they take to un-puff?

WILSON: I don't know. It's not the sort of thing you time.
COOPER: Go home, Wilson.
[*He eases his back.*]
WILSON: You're stiff.
COOPER: I've been sitting down all day. And take that tray with you.
WILSON: Am I un-puffed yet?
COOPER: Beautifully.
WILSON: I feel a fool.
COOPER: Make love.
WILSON: I'll see you Tuesday.
[*She goes, taking the tray with her.*]
COOPER: A brisk walk, that's the thing.
[*He tries to lever himself out of his chair but he can't manage it. He slumps back.*]
Gosh, I enjoyed that. I've got Wilson's tears on my trousers. 'Blessed are the trousers...' Why did Julia never cry on my knee? I can't really remember her crying at all, but she must have done. When? She fell off her little tricycle — yes, she cried then. That's it — I picked her up and she cried on my shoulder. Of course, if I'd wanted her to cry on my knee, I suppose I could have dangled her upside down. I don't remember her crying for sorrow, though — only pain. If I ever find out that Wilson's young man isn't kind... I'll what? Yes, I'll tell George Hartley that Wilson's young man has just kicked over his sand-castle. Strapping chap, George Hartley. And Wilson cried for him. But I've got the tears on my trousers.
[*He has been getting progressively more drowsy. He gives in to it and goes to sleep in his chair. The lights are taken down. When they come up it is almost dark outside.* AYLOTT *comes in and switches on the light.*]
AYLOTT: Cooper?
[COOPER *does not move.*]
[*anxiously*] Cooper?
COOPER: Um? Ah, Aylott. How are you?
AYLOTT: Oh, much the same — mustn't grumble. How are you?
COOPER: Oh, much the same — mustn't grumble. Except that I'm damn near peeing myself.

## ACT ONE, SCENE TWO 35

AYLOTT: Going to the lavatory might be a good idea.
COOPER: I know that, you fool! It's a question of getting up.
AYLOTT: Oh, I see, yes.
  [*He helps* COOPER *out of the chair. It is not easy.*]
COOPER: Come on, come on! Wilson would pluck me out of this chair as though I were a feather.
AYLOTT: Well, you're not.
COOPER: What's that programme?
AYLOTT: What programme?
COOPER: On television, where they play stupid games. 'It's a Knock-Out,' that's it.
AYLOTT: What about it?
COOPER: If they ever do a geriatric version, this would make a wonderful game. 'Get the old man to the lavatory before he pees himself.' Ahh!
AYLOTT: You haven't, have you?
COOPER: No. That was a roar of triumph at standing up.
AYLOTT: Do you want a hand?
COOPER: Certainly not.
  [*He makes his way into the bathroom.*]
AYLOTT: I'm not going to sing.
COOPER: [*going in*] Don't then.
AYLOTT: Chess?
COOPER: [*off*] If you like.
  [AYLOTT *goes and gets a chess-board and pieces. He brings them back to the table and starts to set them up.*]
AYLOTT: How was the visit?
COOPER: [*off*] What I'm doing at the moment describes it rather well.
AYLOTT: Oh.
COOPER: [*off*] How was the walk?
AYLOTT: I went to the sweet-shop — bought some wine-gums. I met a punk.
COOPER: [*off*] A what?
AYLOTT: A punk.
COOPER: [*off*] Did he mug you?
AYLOTT: No, he saw me across the road.
COOPER: [*off*] I expect he'll get you next time.
AYLOTT: What?
  [COOPER *comes out of the bathroom.*]
COOPER: Well, that was an anti-climax. I was expecting a Niagara effect.

AYLOTT: Little and often.
COOPER: Yes. I'll stand up for a bit if you don't mind.
AYLOTT: Of course not. You won't mind if I sit down?
COOPER: No. Only don't get stiff, or by the time I want to sit down you'll have to get up to stretch your legs.
AYLOTT: A yo-yo effect.
COOPER: We'd need the board to be on some sort of hydraulic. Move it up and down for us.
AYLOTT: Then if Wilson came in and asked us how we were, we could say, 'Oh, up and down, up and down.'
  [*They both laugh at this.*]
COOPER: She's off till Tuesday, you know.
AYLOTT: Yes, I know.
COOPER: You're not claiming that she sought you out specially to tell you that, are you?
AYLOTT: No. I met her as I was coming back from my walk. She was running.
COOPER: Home to her young man.
AYLOTT: Lucky young man.
COOPER: What would say to a glass of whisky?
AYLOTT: [*a familiar joke*] Hello whisky.
COOPER: Good man.
  [*He searches in his bedside locker for the whisky and two glasses.*]
  You didn't happen to see George Hartley on your travels, did you?
AYLOTT: No, I don't think so. Why?
COOPER: I just wondered if he knew.
AYLOTT: Knew what?
COOPER: It doesn't matter.
  [*He pours two whiskies.*]
AYLOTT: I didn't see him.
COOPER: You said that.
AYLOTT: I know.
COOPER: [*giving* AYLOTT *his whisky*] There you are.
AYLOTT: Thank you.
  [COOPER *puts down his own whisky on the table and lowers himself into his chair.*]
COOPER: They do have hydraulic armchairs, don't they?
AYLOTT: I haven't seen one here.
COOPER: I wonder if they hiss like the brakes on those big lorries?

## ACT ONE, SCENE TWO

AYLOTT: I think they're electrically powered.
COOPER: I'd prefer hydraulics. Think of the possibilities, especially if you had very powerful ones. For example, if I were ready to go to bed and I was sitting in my hydraulic chair, I could just point the thing in the right direction, press a button and catapult myself right across the room.
AYLOTT: You'd have to be terribly accurate.
COOPER: I'll work on it. 'Cooper's hydraulic aid for the Aged.'

[*They toast each other.*]

The Escape Committee!
AYLOTT: The Escape Committee!
COOPER: [*looking at the board*] You've given me white.
AYLOTT: I'm better than you are.
COOPER: Oh, all right.

[*They begin to play and continue to do so. There is no great concentration and the play is slow.*]

AYLOTT: Why are you so stiff?
COOPER: Would you believe excessive sexual activity?
AYLOTT: No.
COOPER: No. Well, if you must know . . .
AYLOTT: I don't *have* to know. I was merely enquiring.
COOPER: If you must know, I fell over.
AYLOTT: Where?
COOPER: Here. Where do you think?
AYLOTT: I'm sorry to hear that.
COOPER: I wasn't best pleased.
AYLOTT: Did anyone see?
COOPER: Not the fall itself. I went solo on that. But unfortunately my daughter and her flat-roofed husband arrived just in time to catch the aftermath.
AYLOTT: Oh Lord.
COOPER: All the way from Milton Keynes to find your father lying on the floor.
AYLOTT: May have been just as well. If you'd hurt yourself and nobody had been here . . .
COOPER: Then I'd have dragged myself heroically to the bell by the bed, summoned Wilson and asked her to rub some exotic salve into my body.
AYLOTT: Could you have got up on your own?
COOPER: No.

AYLOTT: Well, if you're going to have a fall, this is the place to have it.
COOPER: Oh absolutely. Shame they can't be regulated, though. One could have mattresses placed in strategic positions.
AYLOTT: I am sorry.
COOPER: That's two falls. Perhaps I should start putting little stickers on my chair.
AYLOTT: You should use your stick.
COOPER: Should I?
AYLOTT: I didn't go to the sweet-shop, you know.
COOPER: You said you did.
AYLOTT: I went the wrong way.
COOPER: Oh.
AYLOTT: I ended up on an industrial estate. Quite interesting in its own way — factories, funny little companies, fork-lift trucks ... but it wasn't the sweet-shop.
COOPER: What about the punk?
AYLOTT: Oh there was a punk. He worked there, I suppose. 'Hello Dad,' he said, 'Lost?'
COOPER: I hope you denied it.
AYLOTT: No. Somehow I didn't feel like denying it.
COOPER: You took a wrong turning, that's all.
AYLOTT: There are no turnings. You go out of the gate and turn left for the sweet-shop — or right, as I have now discovered, for an industrial estate.
COOPER: At least you know what's in the other direction.
AYLOTT: But I wanted to go to the sweet-shop.
COOPER: Have another drink.
   [*They both somehow expect the bottle to be on the table, but* COOPER *left it on top of his bedside locker.*]
   Ah. Now if I had my hydraulic chair ...
AYLOTT: I'll get it.
   [*He gets up and goes to fetch the bottle.*]
COOPER: Don't lose your way.
AYLOTT: In future I shall equip myself with distress flares.
   [*He pours them two more drinks. They toast.*]
   The Escape Committee!
COOPER: The Escape Committee!
AYLOTT: What will you do when we get to Switzerland?

COOPER: I shan't ski. I shan't be a member of the Civil Service again, either. I think I'll become a poet and meet a girl who bears a remarkable resemblance to Marjorie. What about you?

AYLOTT: Oh, I shall ski. I could, you know. I think I'd like to work in a small town — not a city. I always rather fancied myself as a watchmaker.

COOPER: Pretty stiff competition in Switzerland.

AYLOTT: I'm not becoming a Zombie, am I, John?

COOPER: Now what sort of question is that?

AYLOTT: One I'd like to answer honestly.

COOPER: I'm not a doctor. Ask Spears.

AYLOTT: You know Spears as well as I do. If you went to see Spears with your head tucked under your arm and asked him if your head had actually come off, he'd 'Ah well' his way through that one.

COOPER: Perhaps if you dropped the head on the floor and kicked it across the room he might commit himself.

AYLOTT: Don't change the subject.

COOPER: You brought Spears up.

AYLOTT: I did not. You brought Spears up, but I'm not asking Spears, I'm asking you.

COOPER: What am I supposed to say?

AYLOTT: Yes or no.

COOPER: There is no 'yes' or 'no'. Good God, just because you went to an industrial estate instead of the sweet-shop . . .

AYLOTT: And I told you twice that I saw Hartley reading a paper in the lounge this morning.

COOPER: Well, you can't be that far gone, can you? All right, you may be getting a bit forgetful, but if you're capable of remembering the things you forgot in the first place, you hardly qualify as a Zombie.

AYLOTT: You admit I'm becoming a bit forgetful then?

COOPER: Yes. All right. Yes.

AYLOTT: Thank you.

COOPER: Not at all.

AYLOTT: You'll tell me if you notice things, won't you?

COOPER: I can hardly maintain a twenty-four hour surveillance.

AYLOTT: When we're together.
COOPER: It's like being asked to spy.
AYLOTT: Check.
COOPER: You old bugger!
AYLOTT: Why?
COOPER: You distract me completely by going on about your poor failing mind, and all the time you're concentrating on the chess.
AYLOTT: I suppose that's rather encouraging.
COOPER: Sharp practice if you ask me. However . . .
  [*He moves a piece.*]
AYLOTT: The funny thing about going in the opposite direction to the sweet-shop was that I didn't even realize the lack of familiar land-marks en route. I did, quite literally, find myself on that industrial estate.
COOPER: What industrial estate?
AYLOTT: The one . . . Oh, very funny. All right, just for that . . . [*moving a piece*] Checkmate.
  [COOPER *accepts the 'Mate' without looking very closely at the board.*]
COOPER: I shall, of course, lodge an official complaint.
AYLOTT: With whom?
COOPER: You.
AYLOTT: Denied.
COOPER: Well, at least I made the gesture. Another game?
AYLOTT: No thanks. To tell the truth I'm a bit tired.
COOPER: Yes, to tell the truth so am I.
AYLOTT: Shall I put this away?
COOPER: No, leave it. I shall re-play the game and find out where I went wrong.
AYLOTT: You didn't play very well, that's what went wrong.
COOPER: You know my inflatable urine bags — the Goodyear airship ones? The first time they fly, they will bear the slogan, 'Aylott is insufferable when he wins at chess!'
AYLOTT: [*getting up*] I'll trundle off then. Do you want a hand before I go?
COOPER: I'd prefer a body. No, I'm all right.
AYLOTT: See you tomorrow, then. Goodnight.
COOPER: Goodnight, Michael.
  [AYLOTT *goes out.*]

COOPER: Industrial estate! 'Can you help me please? I'm in a rather confused estate.' Just a lapse. He'll get his wine-gums tomorrow. Just a lapse. Sounds like one of Spears' 'Ah wells.' [*leaning over the board*] Now let's see. I usually give Aylott a better game than that. Oh Aylott! You'd been playing with your black bishop on a white square and you hadn't noticed. But then, come to think of it, neither had I.

    [*He laughs softly to himself. It is not a very humorous laugh.*]

## END OF ACT ONE

# ACT TWO

## SCENE ONE

*The first Sunday of the next month.*

*COOPER, wearing pyjamas, dressing gown and slippers, comes out of his bathroom.*

*His breakfast tray is on the table, the breakfast half-eaten.*

COOPER: Well, I know something's up. Something must be up to jog the well-oiled Panzer machine out of gear. Of course, it takes an experienced Resistance Fighter to notice, but I know Wilson's on today, so why didn't she bring me my breakfast? Nurse Chatterton brought it — bony girl. Perhaps the whole Division has been replaced — sent to the Russian Front for not oiling their trolleys.

[*He goes to the window and looks out.*]

Looks normal enough.

[WILSON *comes in.*]

WILSON: You didn't eat much breakfast, did you?

COOPER: How could I? For all I know you may have been drawing winter clothing from The Stores.

WILSON: What *are* you talking about?

COOPER: Something's up, isn't it?

[WILSON *makes his bed and replaces the carafe of water by the bedside.*]

WILSON: No.

COOPER: Come on, Wilson. This is me you're talking to, not George Hartley.

WILSON: All right, if you must know. Colonel Bruton died early this morning.

COOPER: I knew something was up.

WILSON: Is that all you've got to say?

COOPER: Well, there's not a lot to add, is there?

WILSON: You could say you were sorry.

COOPER: I could, but it would be quite meaningless. I'm sorry if you were involved, of course, but that's all. Living under one roof doesn't make us a happy band of brothers. Did he die in his sleep?

## ACT TWO, SCENE ONE

WILSON: Yes.
COOPER: I hope he was lying to attention.
WILSON: Mr. Cooper!
COOPER: Sorry. Lovely way to go, that — 'Died in his sleep. Passed peacefully away.' It's not often like that, is it?
WILSON: You'd be surprised.
COOPER: I doubt it. I didn't see the hearse.
WILSON: It came to the side entrance.
COOPER: The Colonel wouldn't have liked that. Gun-carriages and muffled drums, that's what he'd have liked. Are there any other military men here?
WILSON: Not that I know of.
COOPER: That makes me the ranking officer. I think you'd better call me Second Lieutenant in future.
WILSON: I shall call you what I've always called you.
COOPER: Which is unprintable?
WILSON: Partly.
COOPER: You're beautiful when you're insulting, Wilson.
   [*This makes her smile.*]
   You've got to let go when we die.
WILSON: I'm being taken out to lunch today.
COOPER: Name him and I'll kill him. I may have to fling myself from the window onto his head to do it, but I'll kill him.
WILSON: My fella.
COOPER: Ah. Is he on strike?
WILSON: No he's not! He's got the day off. He's calling for me. Why don't I bring him up to meet you?
COOPER: Basically, you're a sexual primitive. You just want to see two men fighting over you, don't you?
WILSON: You'd like him.
COOPER: So you say.
WILSON: You would.
COOPER: Take him to see Aylott.
WILSON: Why?
COOPER: Because I think Aylott presents the more acceptable face of senility.
WILSON: I keep telling you, you're not senile.
COOPER: You know Spears came to see me yesterday?
WILSON: Mr. Spears, yes.
COOPER: Well, ask him.

WILSON: I'll bet you anything you like that he didn't use the word 'senile.'
COOPER: Oh, he didn't *use* it. That would be like swearing in front of the children. But I'll tell you this. I actually caught some words in between all the 'Ah wells.' Phrases even — like 'At your time of life . . . a measure of physical deterioration . . .'
WILSON: Only a measure.
COOPER: An inch or a yard? What's the other chap's name — the one we don't have to call 'Mister?'
WILSON: Doctor O'Loughlin.
COOPER: Yes, him. He doesn't 'Ah well,' I'll give him that, but he will insist on comparing the human body to a car engine. I half expect him to jack me up before he examines me. Talking of jacks, did I tell you of my idea for a hydraulic chair?
WILSON: Will you meet my fella or not?
COOPER: No I won't.
WILSON: Why not?
COOPER: Because I'd want him to like me.
WILSON: That's the first time I've ever heard you say that you want somebody to like you.
COOPER: Only because I love you, Wilson. I'd want him to see what a joy I am, what a charmer, what a merry old soul you have in your care. But I'd try too hard, I know I would. I'd come across as an unnaturally cheerful old loon.
WILSON: He's not a fool.
COOPER: He can't be if he's living with you.
WILSON: Just be yourself.
COOPER: Show him Aylott.
WILSON: I don't want to *show* him anybody!
COOPER: And where's that Baker woman?
WILSON: Why?
COOPER: Because it's the first Sunday in the month, and if the Milton Keynes contingent find me living in squalor, there'll be hell to pay!
WILSON: All right. Meet him another time.
COOPER: Yes.
WILSON: I shan't forget. Now is there anything you want?
COOPER: Yes. Could you bring me back some wine-gums please?

## ACT TWO, SCENE ONE

WILSON: I didn't know you liked wine-gums.
COOPER: There are a lot of things you don't know about me, Wilson.
WILSON: Probably just as well.
COOPER: Probably. Where's your young man taking you for lunch?
WILSON: A pub, I expect.
COOPER: Pshaw!
WILSON: Pardon?
COOPER: Pshaw! P.S.H.A.W. It's a word I used to read a lot in novels but I've never actually said. A pub! Why doesn't he take you down to Brighton and buy you champagne and oysters at Sheekey's?
WILSON: I only get an hour.
COOPER: And what is the cheerful Mrs. Simmons giving *us* for lunch?
WILSON: Chicken or cod.
COOPER: Which do you recommend?
WILSON: The chicken.
COOPER: I'll have the chicken, then.
WILSON: I'll see you later. [*stopping at the door*] Didn't you dream about me last night?
COOPER: Of course.
WILSON: And?
COOPER: ... except for a black velvet band at the neck.
    [WILSON *smiles and goes.*]
    A brisk walk, I think.
    [*He goes to the window.*]
    I feel a bit sorry for the old Colonel, being sneaked out of the side entrance like that. I suppose they were afraid that the sight of a hearse at the front door might induce mass hysteria — or mass heart attacks. I only spoke to the man once or twice. He stopped attending regimental reunions once he moved in here, I know that. Somebody told me. Sheer vanity, of course. Good for you, Colonel.
    [MRS. BAKER *comes in to clean the room.*]
MRS. BAKER: Morning. Shan't be a minute.
COOPER: 'Soft! What light from yonder window breaks ...?'
MRS. BAKER: 'It is the East and Juliet is the sun!' [*triumphantly*] That shut you up, didn't it?
COOPER: Temporarily.

MRS. BAKER: Yes, well.
COOPER: 'Yes, well' what?
MRS. BAKER: I looked it up. I can read. I mean, people like me can read.
COOPER: I've never questioned your literacy.
MRS. BAKER: Not that I get much time for it.
COOPER: You're a terrible snob, Mrs. Baker.
MRS. BAKER: You can't be a snob looking upwards — anybody knows that.
COOPER: Looking upwards at me?
MRS. BAKER: You don't know how lucky you are.
COOPER: You're not going to give me the dirt sandwiches for dinner routine again, are you?
MRS. BAKER: We never go short.
COOPER: You really can't have it both ways, you know.
MRS. BAKER: I've never said anything about dirt sandwiches. I've had Brian at home all week as well. He never gets colds like ordinary kids. His go on and on.
COOPER: What about your father?
MRS. BAKER: What about him?
COOPER: Well, how is he?
MRS. BAKER: You've never asked after him before.
COOPER: Perhaps I'm mellowing.
MRS. BAKER: He doesn't get waited on hand and finger like you, I'll tell you that for nothing.
COOPER: It's certainly not information I'd pay for.
MRS. BAKER: Well, that shows there's some things you can't buy, doesn't it?
COOPER: Does it?
MRS. BAKER: You know what I mean.
COOPER: I hate to admit it, Mrs. Baker, but I don't. You've lost me completely.
MRS. BAKER: Well, there you are. Poor Colonel Bruton passed away this morning.
COOPER: Yes, I know.
MRS. BAKER: Military pension.
COOPER: Is there more to that sentence?
MRS. BAKER: That's all that paid for this. He didn't have a private income.
COOPER: Oh, I see. And you think I do?
MRS. BAKER: Well, you must have — or means.

COOPER: 'Means,' Mrs. Baker, are an entirely different kettle of fish.
MRS. BAKER: You have got them though, haven't you?
COOPER: Yes, and you want to know how.
MRS. BAKER: It's none of my business.
COOPER: No it isn't, but I wouldn't want you dying of curiosity. Dying, that's where it started. My daughter was 24 when her mother died — already married and with child as the Bible would have it. I was 52. I felt older. 'Come to us,' the said. They meant it. But where would that have led — a grandfather annexe in Milton Keynes? I retired at 60. All my savings and the sale of a three-bedroomed house in Merton Park are my 'means,' Mrs. Baker — used, quite consciously, to have myself looked after. And because I pay to be looked after, I don't have to think of myself as a burden to anyone. I don't have to try to be a dear old man and above all I no longer have to live in a house which doesn't have Marjorie in it. My means don't justify my end. They uncomplicate it.

[*He goes into the bathroom.*]

Would you mind singing?
MRS. BAKER: I'm not embarrassed. My father uses a pot.
COOPER: [*off*] In public?
MRS. BAKER: He can't always get there in time.

[MRS. BAKER *sings 'Alice Blue Gown.' She sings softly and it is less for* COOPER *than herself.* COOPER *comes out of the bathroom and stands in the doorway.* MRS. BAKER *does not notice him until she finishes the song.*]

That's his favourite song.
COOPER: Mine's 'The Ball of Kerrymuir.'
MRS. BAKER: I thought it might be.
COOPER: Does your father like whisky?
MRS. BAKER: Yes.

[COOPER *takes a full bottle from his bedside locker and gives it to* MRS. BAKER.]

COOPER: Give him my best. Go on.
MRS. BAKER: You don't know him.
COOPER: I do.

[MRS. BAKER *takes the bottle.*]

MRS. BAKER: I'm sorry about your wife.

COOPER: She used to sing a lot.

MRS. BAKER: Did she have a nice voice?

COOPER: Awful — always off-key — very enthusiastic, though. [*looking out of the window*] Is that wire netting they're putting round the pond?

[MRS. BAKER *joins him at the window.*]

MRS. BAKER: Looks like it.

COOPER: George Hartley hasn't . . . ?

MRS. BAKER: Not that I know of.

COOPER: In case he tries again, I suppose. Or sets a fashion.

MRS. BAKER: He mostly goes down to the orchard now.

COOPER: Let's hope he doesn't start climbing trees.

MRS. BAKER: Now why would he climb trees?

COOPER: Scrumping. Good heavens, the world has come to life this morning. There's a taxi now.

MRS. BAKER: You're like James Stewart in 'Rear Window' you are.

COOPER: Except I've got a front window. I say you fellows, it's a new boy!

MRS. BAKER: Looks like it.

COOPER: Not too steady on his pins. Who's that with him?

MRS. BAKER: How should I know?

COOPER: His sister.

MRS. BAKER: How do you know?

COOPER: Well, they've got the same faces but she's got longer hair.

MRS. BAKER: So they have. He's got a lot of luggage.

COOPER: Some people need a lot of luggage to pack their lives in.

[*Behind them,* AYLOTT *appears in the doorway. He sees* MRS. BAKER, *looks somewhat puzzled and goes, without either of them seeing him.*]

MRS. BAKER: Who brought you in?

COOPER: I was delivered as a registered parcel. Nobody *brought* me in. You don't have the Home Secretary's number, do you?

MRS. BAKER: What are you going on about now?

COOPER: Well, it's a bit much, isn't it? The poor old Colonel's hardly been carted out the side entrance

## ACT TWO, SCENE ONE

before they whisk somebody else into his room through the front entrance.

MRS. BAKER: No, he'll be in Fourteen. There's all the Colonel's things to be cleared out first.

COOPER: Do you — did you clean the Colonel's room?

MRS. BAKER: No. Mrs. Malik.

COOPER: Did she call him 'Colonel Sahib?'

MRS. BAKER: Not to his face.

COOPER: Well, they've gone in to be welcomed by our full-breasted Matron.

MRS. BAKER: I thought you'd been clean for too long.

COOPER: Well, it's spring — the sap's rising.

MRS. BAKER: Here, I shall get shot.

COOPER: Nonsense. A brief passionate dalliance with a resident? Severe reprimand at the most.

MRS. BAKER: I'm talking about getting on.

[*She gathers up her equipment, including the whisky.*]

My dad will like the whisky.

COOPER: Tell him . . .

MRS. BAKER: Tell him what?

COOPER: Give him my best.

MRS. BAKER: Yes I will. Is your daughter coming today?

COOPER: 'Fraid so.

MRS. BAKER: Can she sing?

COOPER: Like a lark.

MRS. BAKER: I'll see you tomorrow, then.

COOPER: Unless I'm out scrumping with Hartley.

MRS. BAKER: It's too early for apples.

COOPER: That won't bother Hartley.

MRS. BAKER: See you tomorrow.

COOPER: 'And yet, by heaven, I think my love as rare
As any she belied with false compare.'

MRS. BAKER: I shall look that up as well.

COOPER: You do, Mrs. Baker.

[MRS. BAKER *goes.* COOPER *looks out of the window again.*]

The taxi's gone. The sister didn't stay long. 'I won't stay long, Percy. You'll only upset yourself.' — something like that. I wonder if he knows where he is yet? When my mother left me on my first day at school, I was quite certain she'd abandoned me.

I suppose the sister will go home now, cook her first lunch for one and wonder if she's done the right thing putting him in here. Nasty expression — 'Putting somebody into a Home' — smacks of violence — struggling old people being carted away. It is violence of a sort. Mrs. Baker won't have her father put away. She'll pretend not to notice the stench of urine and go on singing 'Alice Blue Gown.' I wonder why she doesn't like carols? And where's Aylott? I sound like a King. 'And where's Aylott?' [*imperiously*] Bring me Aylott! Send Aylott to the King! [*echoing*] Send Aylott to the King! Send Aylott to the King!

[MRS. BAKER *comes back in.*]

MRS. BAKER: Are you all right?
COOPER: Of course I'm all right.
MRS. BAKER: I heard you shouting along the corridor.
COOPER: I was wondering where Aylott's got to.
MRS. BAKER: You've got a perfectly good bell by your bed.
COOPER: I wasn't summoning assistance. I was wondering where Aylott was.
MRS. BAKER: Why were you shouting, then?
COOPER: I was just ... It doesn't matter.
MRS. BAKER: You gave me a turn.
COOPER: You mean you actually started spinning round and round in the corridor?
MRS. BAKER: I've got better things to do.
COOPER: Yes, I suppose spinning round and round in a corridor isn't really that productive.
MRS. BAKER: Than be at your beck and call, I mean.
COOPER: I did not beck or call you. I just wondered where Aylott had got to. He's usually popped in by now.
MRS. BAKER: I don't know, do I? Perhaps he's gone for a walk. Now do you mind if I get on?
COOPER: No, no, you get on, Mrs. Baker. If Mohammed won't come to the mountain ...
MRS. BAKER: You mean you're going to look for him?
COOPER: Yes I do.
MRS. BAKER: You're actually going to move outside this room?
COOPER: To the gate if necessary.
MRS. BAKER: About time, some would say.
COOPER: Would they?

## ACT TWO, SCENE ONE

MRS. BAKER: You'll be careful?
COOPER: I shan't run.
MRS. BAKER: No, well, just don't try. And take your stick.
COOPER: I shan't need a stick. If you've polished the corridor floors with your usual thoroughness I shall be able to get to the end of the corridor in one long skid.
MRS. BAKER: Well, mind how you go.
COOPER: I'll give you a wave as I whizz past.

[MRS. BAKER *goes, not entirely approvingly.*]

Shoes, I think, yes.

[*He goes to his wardrobe and takes out his shoes. He kicks off his slippers and waggles his feet into his shoes. For one self-delusory moment he considers putting a foot on a chair to tie the laces, but discretion gets the better part of valour and he sits to tie his laces. This is not an easy task in itself and it leaves him a little out of breath.*]

Well, that's a good start, isn't it?

[*He takes a walking stick from the wardrobe. He looks at it with distaste.*]

'Just to give you confidence,' the physiotherapist said.

[*Quite deliberately he puts the stick over his shoulder as he goes to the door and opens it. He puts the stick to the floor immediately.*]

Well, come on, confidence.

[*He goes slowly out into the corridor.*]


## SCENE TWO

*Later that afternoon.*

COOPER *is asleep in his chair.* JULIA *pops her head round the door.*

JULIA: Cooee!

[COOPER *does not stir.* JULIA *comes in, followed by* PETER. *They look at each other and then at* COOPER *— worried. They tip-toe close to make sure that he is breathing.*]

[*softly*] Dad?

> [COOPER *does not stir.* JULIA *and* PETER *make small, vague, enquiring gestures to one another, then* JULIA *sits in the other armchair.* PETER *starts his walkabout, which annoys her. She gestures irritably and he brings over a straight-backed chair and sits on it. After a little silence,* PETER *begins to tap his knee and 'pom-pom' softly to himself. Another gesture from* JULIA *puts a stop to this.* COOPER *stirs. They lean forward expectantly but he shows signs of going back to sleep again.*]

Dad?
COOPER: What?
JULIA: We're here.
> [COOPER *wakes up.*]
COOPER: What's the time?
JULIA: I'm afraid we're rather late. How are you?
COOPER: Oh, much the same — mustn't grumble. How long have you been here?
JULIA: Not long. You were asleep, you see.
PETER: I see you've got your shoes on.
COOPER: I must give you full marks for your powers of observation.
JULIA: You haven't even said 'Hello.'
COOPER: Hello. Well?
JULIA: Oh! Hello, Dad.
PETER: Hello, Dad.
COOPER: You never did tell me what the time was?
PETER: Half three.
COOPER: That's odd.
PETER: It's those roadworks, I'm afraid. We got off at Junction 11 and rejoined at 9 to avoid them, but they're further down today.
COOPER: The whole day's out of gear.
JULIA: Peter's just explained that.
COOPER: Here, I mean. It's that damn Colonel's fault for dying.
> [JULIA *and* PETER *look at each other, concerned as to his mental state.* COOPER *realizes.*]
[*deliberately*] One of the residents died this morning.

## ACT TWO, SCENE TWO

PETER: Oh. I am sorry.
COOPER: Why? You didn't know him.
PETER: Well no, but one man's death diminishes us all, doesn't it?
COOPER: I don't feel diminished. I do want to pee, though.
PETER: Shall I . . . ?
JULIA: Give Dad a hand.
　　　　　[PETER *helps* COOPER *up.*]
COOPER: Why do you always pull? You'll find yourself holding an arm with a soggy stump one of these days. That's it.
　　　　　[*He goes into the bathroom.*]
JULIA: I knew he was going to be difficult today. I had a feeling.
PETER: He doesn't look very well, does he?
JULIA: Shh!
PETER: Well, he doesn't.
　　　　　[*The door from the corridor opens and* AYLOTT *stands there.*]
AYLOTT: Sorry.
JULIA: Good afternoon.
AYLOTT: It's Sunday, isn't it?
PETER: That's right.
AYLOTT: Where's Cooper?
JULIA: He's in the bathroom. I'm his daughter.
AYLOTT: Well, he wasn't here before.
PETER: Was he not?
AYLOTT: I'm Aylott. My name is Aylott.
JULIA: Father's friend. We've heard a lot about you. [*calling*] Dad! Your friend's here.
COOPER: [*off*] Aylott?
AYLOTT: Cooper?
　　　　　[COOPER *comes out of the bathroom.*]
　　　　　Where have you been?
COOPER: Where have *you* been?
JULIA: Why don't we all sit down?
AYLOTT: No thank you. I'll see you later, Cooper. Sorry. Thank you.
　　　　　[AYLOTT *closes the door.* COOPER *looks a little concerned.*]
PETER: What was all that about?

JULIA: Peter! He seems very nice, Dad, your friend Mr. Aylott.
COOPER: Is he going off his trolley or am I?
JULIA: No-one's going off his trolley. There was obviously a mix-up.
PETER: He said you weren't here before.
COOPER: I was looking for him.
JULIA: Out?
COOPER: Well, I didn't expect to find him in the wardrobe.
PETER: Well, that's it, isn't it? You went to look for him. He came to look for you and you obviously missed each other.
COOPER: There's a lot of the Hercules Poirot about you. I realize what happened this afternoon, but where was he this morning?
PETER: We don't know that, do we?
COOPER: [*frustrated*] No.
JULIA: You can sort it all out when you see him later.
COOPER: Yes.

[*He sits down.* JULIA *sits in the armchair.* PETER *brings a straight-backed chair and sits on that.*]

I think you're right about not bringing Gary.
JULIA: He sends his love.
PETER: And he said to tell you that he'll give you Benaud if you give him Trueman instead of Lindwall.
COOPER: How are the nightmares?
JULIA: They've stopped.

[*This means that they haven't brought Gary anyway and they all know it.*]

COOPER: And how was the A.5. this month?
PETER: Horrendous.
COOPER: Good.
JULIA: Dad!
COOPER: Daughter!
JULIA: Look, we don't come to see you for our sakes, you know.
COOPER: Then don't come. You don't do me any good.
JULIA: That's a hateful thing to say!
COOPER: It's the truth. I can see your martyred expressions as you get into the car at Milton Keynes. 'First Sunday in the month again — doesn't it come round quickly? Oh well, let's get it over with.' And

## ACT TWO, SCENE TWO

you bring your martyrdom in here with you like a big black cloud.
JULIA: We've never complained to you.
COOPER: No, you take it out on the M.1. instead.
PETER: It is a factor.
COOPER: My God, don't I know it's a factor? I'm beginning to think that I know every roadworks on the damn thing!
JULIA: You don't make it easy. You don't even try.
COOPER: What do you expect me to do? Lay on a tea dance?
JULIA: Sarcasm. It's always sarcasm, isn't it? I tell you this. I don't know how Peter stands it.
[PETER *is somewhat taken aback to be used like this.*]
COOPER: Let's ask him. How do you stand it, Peter?
PETER: I make allowances.
COOPER: You see, he makes allowances.
JULIA: Well, he shouldn't have to. There's nothing wrong with your mind. There's no reason why we can't hold a normal conversation.
COOPER: All right, let's talk about the M.1. if you want to.
JULIA: I don't want to talk about the M.1!
COOPER: Well, what else is there? That's the only thing that seems to join us.
PETER: That's not entirely our fault, is it? You don't show any interest in our lives at all.
COOPER: And you're bored with hearing about mine?
PETER: I didn't say that.
JULIA: Well, perhaps you should have.
PETER: Come on now, Julia.
JULIA: And stop trying to be so bloody reasonable all the time! [*to* COOPER] There's nothing to your life except the past — nothing interesting, but all you'll ever talk about is now — here.
COOPER: Because I refuse to become one of those boring old farts whose every sentence begins with, 'I remember.'
JULIA: So you tell us who's died, who's had a stroke, who's gone off his head . . .
COOPER: That *is* my news.
PETER: Why don't you let us take you for a drive one Sunday?
COOPER: With a blanket over my knees presumably?

PETER: If you wanted one.
JULIA: Peter, I've left Dad's present in the car. Would you go and fetch it please?
PETER: Yes, all right.
   [*He goes out.*]
JULIA: And I don't like Peter being humiliated.
COOPER: I just tickle him up sometimes. There's no harm done. He doesn't even notice.
JULIA: He's a good man.
COOPER: I'm sure he is.
JULIA: He's a good father, too.
COOPER: Gary's a bit like him, isn't he?
JULIA: Yes he is. He's a devil sometimes.
COOPER: Good-oh. You were a good little girl, you know. Everyone used to say how good you were.
JULIA: I made a conscious effort. I wanted to please you.
COOPER: You did.
JULIA: But I never got close.
COOPER: It's a fallacy you know, that a daughter is always her father's girl.
JULIA: I didn't get close to either of you. You always seemed so complete, you and Mum. I never thought that you didn't want me, I'm not saying that, but I never felt that you needed me either. I don't feel that you need me even now.
COOPER: You're not going to cry, are you?
JULIA: No.
COOPER: I do, you know. If . . .
JULIA: If what?
COOPER: 'Big boys don't cry,' you see. Even when you graze your knees, someone always picks you up and says, 'You're not going to cry, are you? Big boys don't cry.' So you don't — or at least you try not to. And it goes on. Do you know, when I was in the Military Hospital in Alexandria, I saw wards full of chaps with burns — bits blown off — blinded — and when the Doctor said to any one of them, 'And how are you today?' do you know what they'd say? 'Fine — very well — not so bad.' They didn't say it because they were heroes. They said it because they thought that they were supposed to say it. And it goes on. 'How are you today, Mr. Cooper?'

## ACT TWO, SCENE TWO

'Oh, much the same — mustn't grumble.' Sometimes I want to say, 'I'm frightened.' I want to say that I'm feeling very sorry for myself — and I want somebody to say they're sorry for me.

JULIA: You could tell me.
COOPER: Just sometimes.
JULIA: Whenever you want.
COOPER: I'm not talking about a three boxes of Kleenex job every month. Just sometimes.
[*They hold hands.*]
JULIA: You still miss Mum.
COOPER: Every day.
JULIA: Look, Jennie starts college in a couple of months' time. It's a nice room — and there's the garden.
COOPER: I'm all right here you know. Ranking Officer as well, now the Colonel's gone to Valhalla — sorry.
[PETER *comes back in. He carries a book.*]
PETER: Sorry. Somebody thought he knew me. Big chap — elderly.
COOPER: That would be Hartley.
PETER: He thought I was his nephew. Then he wanted to know if his blue suit had come back from the cleaners.
COOPER: Yes, that's Hartley all right. Look here, Peter, I do appreciate you coming all this way every month. You mustn't take me seriously.
PETER: [*taken aback*] Oh.
COOPER: I've decided to mellow.
JULIA: Dad might come and stay with us for a while when Jennie goes to college.
PETER: Oh yes?
COOPER: My God, I do admire your control of the facial muscles.
JULIA: Just for a week or two.
COOPER: See here, Julia, I don't think we should gild the lily, do you?
JULIA: [*understanding*] No. Perhaps not.
PETER: You'd be very welcome.
COOPER: Thank you. Now where's my present?
[PETER *hands* COOPER *the book.* COOPER *is delighted.*]
COOPER: Oh, I say. Wisden. Thank you. It's 1947!

PETER: I know. They're out of print but I managed to hunt one down. That Middlesex team you always talk about — they're in there. And the name you can never remember — the eleventh player . . .
COOPER: No, don't tell me!
JULIA: Dad wants to look it up for himself.
COOPER: No I don't.
PETER: But that's why I hunted the book down.
JULIA: It took ages.
COOPER: And I'm very grateful but you see, trying to think of that eleventh name occupies Aylott and I for hours.
PETER: You mean you'll never look it up?
COOPER: One day. And thanks to you I shall be able to.
JULIA: I don't understand.
COOPER: Well, you've got to have a challenge, haven't you? I mean, the Atlantic's been rowed, Everest has been climbed — and as Aylott can't swim and I don't like heights they're out anyway. So we settle for the eleventh name. [*patting the book*] And it's in there.
PETER: But you won't look?
COOPER: One day.
PETER: [*not seeing*] I see.
COOPER: Listen! Panzers!

[PETER *and* JULIA *don't like the sound of this.*]
The tea-trolley.
PETER: Good Lord, is that the time?
JULIA: We could stay for tea.
PETER: Yes, we could.
COOPER: Better not to. You have to order in advance, you see — could cause all sorts of administrative problems.
PETER: Oh well, in that case . . .
JULIA: It can't be that difficult to find two extra cups.
COOPER: The sandwiches are pretty curly as well.
PETER: We did tell Mother we'd be home by seven.
COOPER: Well, there you are. How's her stomach by the way?
PETER: Oh, it's eased off considerably, thank you.
COOPER: Good.
JULIA: We could always ring her.
COOPER: Julia!

## ACT TWO, SCENE TWO

JULIA: What?
COOPER: Let's end the day on a winning note.
JULIA: All right. We'll see you next month, then.
PETER: Perhaps we could go for that car ride.
COOPER: Only if I can ride in the front.
PETER: That's the spirit. Cheerio then, Dad.
COOPER: Thank you for the Wisden. Give Gary my love — and tell him that I'll take Benaud and give him Trueman, but I'm still not convinced about Knott instead of Evans.
PETER: Right. Cheerio, then.
COOPER: Cheerio, Peter. Good luck with the M.1.
PETER: Thank you.

[JULIA *goes to* COOPER, *puts her arms round him and hugs him.*]

JULIA: Goodbye, Dad.
COOPER: Goodbye, dear.

[JULIA *follows* PETER *quite quickly.* COOPER *sits for a moment, then gets up.*]

A brisk walk, I think.

[*He stretches his legs round the room.*]

Sid Brown, Jack Robertson, Bill Edrich, Denis Compton, Dewes, Mann, Leslie Compton, Jim Sims, Jack Young and Laurie Gray. It's still ten.

[*He picks up the Wisden then puts it down again.*]

Temptation, thy name is Wisden!

[WILSON *comes in with a tea-tray. There are two cups and saucers on it.*]

Look here, Wilson, would you keep this book for me?
WILSON: Why?
COOPER: I'm afraid I'll crib.
WILSON: Are you taking some sort of cricket examination?
COOPER: Sort of. I know. Keep it in the same drawer as those stockings you might wear in the summer — make the temptation even more delicious.
WILSON: Come and have your tea.
COOPER: I don't want any tea.

[WILSON *sets the tray down. She sits and starts to eat and drink.*]

Look here, this isn't the station buffet, you know.
WILSON: I'm starving.

COOPER: Well, leave *some*.
  [*He sits and joins her for tea.*]
  How you can sit there feeding your face when there are poor hungry old men feeling faint for lack of nourishment, I don't know.
WILSON: You're the last. You're the end room.
COOPER: If our full-breasted Matron catches you ...
WILSON: I shall say that this is the only way I can get you to eat your tea.
COOPER: You'd betray me as easily as that?
WILSON: Oh yes. Why have you got your shoes on?
COOPER: Why does my footwear assume so much importance round here?
WILSON: Would you like your slippers?
COOPER: No.
  [WILSON *gets his slippers.*]
  I went for a walk, if you must know.
WILSON: [*concerned*] On your own?
COOPER: Except for twenty Sherpas. I was looking for Aylott. He didn't turn up this morning. Then the old fool did turn up — slap in the middle of visiting. Is he all right?
  [WILSON *changes* COOPER's *shoes for his slippers.*]
WILSON: You didn't find him this morning, then?
COOPER: I didn't find anybody. I set up Base Camp at the foot of the stairs — then slogged on as far as the first seat in the garden. Then I ran out of oxygen.
WILSON: You haven't been out for a long time. You should have taken it easily.
COOPER: I did! It took me half an hour to get that far. Did you get those wine-gums?
WILSON: Would I dare not to?
  [*She produces a bag from her pocket and gives them to* COOPER.]
COOPER: They're for Aylott. I've half a mind not to give them to him. Silly old fool! You didn't tell me if he was all right.
WILSON: Yes.
COOPER: That 'yes' lacks conviction.
COOPER: Well — apparently he had a bit of a rough do this morning.

COOPER: What sort of 'rough do?' What does that mean? Were you there?
WILSON: No.
COOPER: Why not?
WILSON: I'm not the only nurse in the place!
COOPER: Sorry.
WILSON: I didn't hear about Mr. Aylott till I got back from lunch.
COOPER: What's wrong with him? What was it?
WILSON: Nothing physical. He just got a little confused.
COOPER: You mean he went off his trolley, don't you?
WILSON: No I don't! He became disoriented. It was just a temporary dislocation.
COOPER: What a nasty little prefix 'dis-' is.
WILSON: It passed.
COOPER: It must have done. I saw him not an hour ago . . . except that he obviously had no idea what the time was.
WILSON: If you see him this evening . . .
COOPER: Go on.
WILSON: Don't ask him about it.
COOPER: It may surprise you to know that I am aware of areas of embarrassment in other people.
WILSON: It's not necessarily a question of embarrassment. He might not remember.
COOPER: Oh. What if he does?
WILSON: What do you think?
COOPER: I shriek with laughter and chant, 'Aylott is a Zombie?'
WILSON: He's not a Zombie. Something like this may not happen again.
COOPER: For some time?
WILSON: Maybe ages.
COOPER: How long's an age at our age? What if he *does* remember, Wilson? What do I do?
WILSON: Be his friend.
COOPER: I am.
WILSON: That's what I mean.
COOPER: I've got an awful feeling that you're relying on my intuition.
WILSON: That's all there is.

COOPER: Then God help Aylott.
[WILSON *starts to put the tea-things back on the tray.*]
Are you going?
WILSON: I'm off.
COOPER: Why do nurses always say that? You make yourself sound like a piece of cod.
WILSON: It's just a ploy, really. It gives patients the opportunity to crack corny jokes.
[*She picks up the tray, but then puts it down again. She draws her chair close to* COOPER *and sits.*]
There's something I want to tell you.
COOPER: Is it some inside dirt on the new chap?
WILSON: I'm going to be married.
COOPER: Oh. When did all this happen?
WILSON: Lunch-time.
COOPER: He didn't propose in the pub?
WILSON: No. On the way back.
COOPER: I hope he stopped the car.
WILSON: He hasn't got a car. He's got a motor-bike.
COOPER: Did he take his crash-helmet off?
WILSON: No.
COOPER: Did you?
WILSON: No.
COOPER: And they say that romance is dead!
WILSON: You haven't said you're pleased.
COOPER: If you're happy, Wilson, of course I'm pleased.
WILSON: You'll have to meet him now.
COOPER: Yes, honour demands it. What shall it be — bedpans at twenty paces?
WILSON: Better make it ten. He's rather short-sighted.
COOPER: Make it thirty, then. What do your parents think?
WILSON: I'm going to phone them tonight. I wanted to tell you first.
COOPER: If I weren't made of granite, a statement like that could un-man me, you know.
WILSON: And I want you to come to the wedding.
COOPER: When will it be?
WILSON: Sometime in the summer.
COOPER: I'll probably have to be wheeled by then. Still, I'll deck the commode with white ribbons and get

## ACT TWO, SCENE TWO

George Hartley to push. I hope there are no ponds on the way.
WILSON: You will come?
COOPER: Perhaps I could be a page boy. Wilson?
WILSON: Yes.
COOPER: [*trying to sound casual*] When will you leave?
WILSON: Who said I was leaving?
COOPER: I thought you might leave to get married.
WILSON: No, of course I shan't.
COOPER: What about babies?
WILSON: Well yes, I expect so — eventually.
COOPER: You're not pregnant now, are you?
WILSON: No I'm not!
COOPER: Bit of a cheek, that.
WILSON: I'd expect no less from you. I must be going. Have you got everything you want?
COOPER: I think so. Quite a day. I've finally made contact — some sort of contact with my daughter, and my other daughter's just told me that she's going to get married.

[WILSON *kisses his cheek.*]

You could get struck off for that. You'll tell me when you *are* pregnant, won't you?
WILSON: Why?
COOPER: So that I can start knitting. Aylott should be here soon.
WILSON: Would you like me to call in on him?
COOPER: No. Leave it to him.
WILSON: You won't let go, will you?
COOPER: You won't.
WILSON: No.
COOPER: Then I shan't.
WILSON: See you tomorrow.
COOPER: Goodnight, dear Wilson. And listen! If anybody dies tomorrow morning, stick them in the freezer and make sure I get my breakfast on time.

[WILSON *goes.*]

You crash-helmeted, short-sighted, not especially good-looking young man. If I were honest, I'd wish a very low sperm-count on you. I expect Wilson would still come to see me — perhaps on the second Sunday in every month. [*seeing the Wisden still on the table*] Oh damn, she forgot the Wisden.

> [*He gets up. He takes the book and puts it in a cupboard.*]

Oh Aylott, if you knew I had a Wisden in my cupboard. When he comes, I'll ... I don't want him to come. I don't want him to come unless he's the proper Aylott. 'Be his friend,' Wilson said. 'I am,' I said. So come ahead, Aylott, whoever you are.

> [*The lights are taken down. When they come up again, it is dark outside and the lights in the room are on.* COOPER *sits in his armchair.*]

Leslie Compton, Jim Sims, Jack Young and Laurie Gray. And it's still ten.

> [*He looks up as he hears a sound at the door.* AYLOTT *comes in.*]

Aylott!
AYLOTT: Cooper!
COOPER: How are you?
AYLOTT: Oh, much the same — mustn't grumble. How are you?
COOPER: Oh, much the same — mustn't grumble.
> [AYLOTT *sits down.*]

What would you say to a glass of whisky?
AYLOTT: Hello whisky.
COOPER: Good man.
> [*He pours them both a glass of whisky. He is looking very closely at* AYLOTT.]

The Escape Committee!
AYLOTT: The Escape Committee!
> [*They sip.*]

Are you all right?
COOPER: Yes. Why?
AYLOTT: You're staring.
COOPER: It's a question of focus. I think I need new glasses.
AYLOTT: He's deaf as a post you know.
COOPER: Who is?
AYLOTT: Whatshisname.
COOPER: I don't know who you're talking about.
AYLOTT: Yes you do. The Optician.
COOPER: Oh.

## ACT TWO, SCENE TWO

AYLOTT: 'Which is clearer now,' he says, 'the green or the red?' 'The red,' you say. 'Pardon?' he says. When I came out last time, I was quite hoarse.

COOPER: It's probably some sort of medical conspiracy. He's probably drumming up trade for a throat specialist.

AYLOTT: Who then gives you some pills with a very tiny label on the bottle — very tiny writing.

COOPER: So you have to go to the Optician's to have your eyes tested again.

AYLOTT: Quite.

[COOPER *is pleased with* AYLOTT's *quickness.*]

COOPER: Well, that's better, isn't it?

AYLOTT: Oh yes. What is?

COOPER: [*off-guard*] Oh . . . life in general.

AYLOTT: Is it?

COOPER: Yes.

AYLOTT: Why?

COOPER: I don't know, it just is! What about a game of chess?

AYLOTT: No, I don't think so. Somebody died this morning, didn't they?

COOPER: It wasn't me. Come on, drink up.

AYLOTT: Somebody died.

COOPER: The Colonel. Colonel Bruston.

AYLOTT: Bruton.

COOPER: Yes, that's it — Bruton.

AYLOTT: It was this morning, wasn't it?

COOPER: Yes. You just said it was this morning.

AYLOTT: I thought I'd be assertive and hope I was right.

COOPER: [*pushing the bag towards him*] I got you some wine-gums.

AYLOTT: That's very kind of you. But you don't go to the sweet-shop.

COOPER: I've invented jet-propelled roller skates.

AYLOTT: You never go to the sweet-shop.

COOPER: Wilson got them for me. Wilson!

AYLOTT: All right, I'm not deaf. I'm quite capable of going there myself, you know.

COOPER: I'll have them back in that case.

[AYLOTT *pushes the bag across the table.*]

I wasn't serious!

AYLOTT: No, if you want them back, you have them back.

COOPER: I don't want them back!
AYLOTT: Well, I don't want them. I'll get my own.
COOPER: Look here, I'm supposed to behave like this, not you.
AYLOTT: And where were you?
COOPER: When?
AYLOTT: This morning.
COOPER: I went to look for you.
AYLOTT: Where was I?
COOPER: I don't know, I couldn't find you! What do you mean, where were you?
AYLOTT: Because I can't remember, Cooper!
COOPER: Oh. Well it's not important is it?
AYLOTT: It's all mixed up.
COOPER: It doesn't matter.
AYLOTT: Of course it matters! Don't patronize me. Of course it matters. I'm afraid.
COOPER: You've just forgotten.
AYLOTT: It's not like a name or a place — it's a whole morning. Why aren't you surprised?
COOPER: I am.
AYLOTT: You know.
COOPER: Well yes, Wilson did mention it.
AYLOTT: Then why didn't you say so?
COOPER: She said you might not remember.
AYLOTT: Remember what I did this morning, or remember that I forgot what I did this morning?
COOPER: Both. I don't know.
AYLOTT: Well, what happened? What did I do?
COOPER: She didn't go into details. You obviously didn't attempt to strangle anybody or streak around the grounds. What did she call it? Just a temporary dislocation.
AYLOTT: Have you ever *seen* a dislocation — a physical dislocation?
COOPER: No. I can't say that I have.
AYLOTT: Well, I have. A chap I played rugby with dislocated his arm. A piece of machinery hinged to bend one way — then quite suddenly it bends the other.
COOPER: It's still only temporary.
AYLOTT: You can't put a plaster cast on your mind, can you?
COOPER: It would look pretty strange.

## ACT TWO, SCENE TWO

AYLOTT: [*suddenly*] I was here.
COOPER: Yes. This afternoon. You met my daughter.
AYLOTT: I know that! Before, I mean. I was here this morning.
COOPER: Oh.
AYLOTT: I was.
COOPER: I could have been in the bathroom. I spend quite a lot of time in the bathroom.
AYLOTT: No. You were talking to somebody.
COOPER: Was I?
AYLOTT: Mrs. Baker! You were talking to Mrs. Baker!
COOPER: Yes, I remember now.
AYLOTT: No you don't. You were talking to Mrs. Baker and neither of you saw me.
COOPER: Ah.
AYLOTT: I've found a way of making myself invisible, you see. You were both looking out of the window, you fool! So I left.
COOPER: You could have had the courtesy to say 'Good morning.'
AYLOTT: No. I was confused. It was as though all the clocks had gone haywire. So I thought, 'I know, I'll talk to Cooper.'
COOPER: Then why didn't you?
AYLOTT: Because Mrs. Baker was here and she confuses me at the best of times. So I went.
COOPER: What happened then, Holmes?
AYLOTT: I went downstairs. There was a coffin.
COOPER: The Colonel.
AYLOTT: Yes.
COOPER: So where were you when I went out to look for you this afternoon?
AYLOTT: I must have been back in my room.
COOPER: Well, this is a fine time to tell me that, isn't it? I could have done myself in wandering about out there.
AYLOTT: Well, anybody with half a mind would have checked to see whether I was in my room first!
COOPER: Anybody with half a mind? That's rich.
AYLOTT: Yes it is, isn't it?
COOPER: What would you say to another whisky?
AYLOTT: Hello another whisky.

COOPER: So would I.
[*He pours them each another glass.*]
AYLOTT: I didn't recognize the moment, you know. I didn't 'feel funny' as Mrs. Baker would put it. I don't even remember waking up this morning.
COOPER: Did you shave?
AYLOTT: [*feeling his face*] Apparently.
COOPER: I think you'd better get a safety razor.
AYLOTT: It's very annoying. My first trip to Zombieland and I don't even know if I enjoyed it.
COOPER: What was it like — the coming back?
AYLOTT: Peculiar.
COOPER: Is that it?
AYLOTT: I couldn't remember the names of things — quite ordinary things. I knew the table was a table, but I simply couldn't think of the name for it. People too — and I couldn't make any sense of the time. I'm ashamed to say I became rather distressed. Wine-gum?
COOPER: No thanks. Grape and grain, you know.
AYLOTT: You're staring at me again.
COOPER: Sorry. A new chap arrived today.
AYLOTT: What's he like?
COOPER: I haven't met him.
AYLOTT: I should chum up with him if I were you.
COOPER: Why?
AYLOTT: Well . . .
COOPER: Oh, don't be so damn silly, Aylott!
AYLOTT: I'd like to think that when I become a fully-fledged Zombie, I should become firm friends with George Hartley, but it doesn't seem to work like that. For some reason, known only to God and Mr. Spears, Zombies don't to seem to share anything except the state of being a Zombie. You'd think they'd be allowed that much, wouldn't you?
COOPER: You sound as though you're about to catch a train.
AYLOTT: Well, I am in a way. The trouble is, I don't know what time it leaves.
COOPER: Shouldn't you be resting?
AYLOTT: [*reprovingly*] Cooper!
COOPER: Just a thought.

## ACT TWO, SCENE TWO

AYLOTT: You'll be saying, 'There are a lot of people worse off than you' next.
COOPER: Or 'You're bound to get out of breath at your age.'
AYLOTT: 'You can't expect to read small print without spectacles . . .'
COOPER: 'You're looking a lot better today. Isn't he looking a lot better today?'
AYLOTT: And the plum. 'I hope I'm as lively as you when I'm your age.' Nobody means that. They think, 'Oh God, is this what I'm going to become?'
COOPER: Spears' 'Ah wells' suddenly sound quite acceptable, don't they?
AYLOTT: He did quite of lot of those this morning. Most of the conversation seemed to be rather a babble, but I definitely picked up a few of Spears' 'Ah wells.'
COOPER: He came to see you, then?
AYLOTT: I think I drew quite a crowd.
COOPER: That's not fair. I could have been breathing my last on that seat in the garden and there wasn't a soul about.
AYLOTT: We might take a stroll together tomorrow.
COOPER: Yes. If I'm going to start going to weddings I shall need to get in trim.
AYLOTT: What weddings?
COOPER: Just weddings.
AYLOTT: Are you telling me that all of a sudden you've been flooded with invitations to a lot of weddings?
COOPER: Yes. Well, one . . .
AYLOTT: Whose?
COOPER: Wilson's. She told me first, you know.
AYLOTT: She's very fond of you. She'll leave.
COOPER: Not until they have a child. She could have done the decent thing and waited till I died.
AYLOTT: 'Lots of good years left though.'
COOPER: The other thing they say is, 'He could go on for years.' That has an altogether nastier ring to it. It contains an implied threat. 'He *could* go on for years.'
AYLOTT: Sounds like a war.
COOPER: Exactly.
AYLOTT: Have a wine-gum.

COOPER: No thank you.
  [AYLOTT *goes to take one himself, but then stares at the bag for a long time.*]
  Are you all right?
AYLOTT: I didn't buy these, did I?
COOPER: No. I got Wilson to get them.
AYLOTT: That's right.
  [*He feels the top of the table with his hand.*]
COOPER: What are you doing?
AYLOTT: It's a cotton-wool feeling — as though there's cotton-wool between the whatsitsname and my fingers.
COOPER: It's pins and needles.
AYLOTT: No. What time is it?
COOPER: Nine o'clock.
AYLOTT: Wilson got the wine-gums.
COOPER: Yes. Wilson.
AYLOTT: Cooper!
COOPER: What? [*Pause.*] What is it?
  [AYLOTT *gets up.*]
  Where are you going? Come and sit down.
  [AYLOTT *obeys quite meekly.*]
  Where were you going?
AYLOTT: I don't know.
COOPER: Oh. Fair enough. Nothing like a short mystery tour. [*talking quickly — to say anything*] Now that's an idea. If we could get hold of a coach, we could run mystery tours from here. We could get Hartley to drive. Marjorie and I used to go coach-riding when we first got married — Sundays mostly — out to the country. Did you ever go for coach-rides, Aylott?
AYLOTT: There isn't a coach.
COOPER: No, not here.
AYLOTT: There was a hearse.
COOPER: This morning.
AYLOTT: What's the time?
COOPER: Look, don't keep worrying about the time. It doesn't matter what time it is. Let's find some calmer waters somewhere.
AYLOTT: Switzerland.
COOPER: What about Switzerland?

AYLOTT: Water. There are beautiful lakes in Switzerland.
COOPER: Yes. Yes, there are.
  [AYLOTT *chuckles*.]
  What?
AYLOTT: I was going to Switzerland.
COOPER: Were you? When was this?
AYLOTT: Not really going — with a friend. We formed an Escape Committee and we made plans to escape to Switzerland — only a game.
COOPER: Don't leave me, Aylott.
AYLOTT: I live here. But everything's made of cotton-wool. Names are made of cotton-wool.
COOPER: Cooper! I'm Cooper!
AYLOTT: That's right.
COOPER: Don't just agree with me, you silly old fart! Do you know I'm Cooper or not?
AYLOTT: [*dully*] Cooper.
  [*He sits back and looks around the room as though he doesn't recognize it.* COOPER *gets up and goes towards the bell by the bed. Then he stops, looks at his groin and laughs bitterly.*]
COOPER: Well, we made it, Aylott. We *did* time it perfectly. No warning — just the first warm trickle. Where's the dignity for us?
  [*He takes up the bell-push on its cord.*]
  'Press button to summon assistance.' But who can they assist? I can change my pyjama trousers and you're quite capable of losing your mind without any help.
  [*He drops the bell-push.*]
  Let's look after ourselves.
  [*He takes a clean pair of pyjamas from his wardrobe.*]
  It's a fitting at the rubber tailor's for me tomorrow. When I go to Wilson's wedding, I hope I don't make sloshing noises as I walk into the church. [*going over to* AYLOTT] You stay there. I'm going to change my nappy. Have another wine-gum.
  [*He pats* AYLOTT'*s arm and goes towards the bathroom.*]
AYLOTT: Cooper?
  [COOPER *turns.*]
COOPER: Aylott?

AYLOTT: There's a team.
COOPER: What sort of team?
AYLOTT: Cricket. Middlesex. 1947.
COOPER: Go on. Don't let go.
AYLOTT: Cotton-wool names.
   [COOPER *finds this more important than changing his trousers. He perches, rather gingerly, on the edge of his armchair.*]
COOPER: Jack Robertson — Sid Brown . . .
AYLOTT: Jack Robertson — Sid Brown . . . Bill Edrich, Denis Compton.
COOPER: You would pick the easy ones, wouldn't you? Well, go on.
AYLOTT: Dewes. Somebody Dewes.
COOPER: George or John. We're never sure.
AYLOTT: But we settle for John.
COOPER: We do. You're right.
AYLOTT: I'm right.
COOPER: F.G. Mann — Leslie Compton . . .
AYLOTT: I was going to say that.
COOPER: Well, you'll have to be quicker, won't you?
AYLOTT: Leslie Compton — as I was about to say.
COOPER: All right, all right! Go on then, clever-socks.
AYLOTT: Leslie Compton . . .
COOPER: Jim . . .
AYLOTT: Sims. [*in a rush*] Jim Sims, Jack Young and Laurie Gray.
COOPER: You did it — the whole team.
AYLOTT: It's still only ten men.
   [COOPER *is vastly relieved to hear this.*]
COOPER: So it is. So it is.
AYLOTT: Do you know something? It occurs to me that we should give in and find some way to look up that eleventh name.
COOPER: Oh no. Not yet, Aylott. Not quite yet.

**CURTAIN**